INJURY, DAMAGE TO HEALTH AND CRUEL TREATMENT

Present Conditions in the Shipment of Live Fauna (1985)

Written & Researched by
John Brookland & Cheryl Hora

Consultant Editor L A 'Nick' Carter

FOREWARD BY SIR PETER SCOTT, CBE DSC

Dedicated to all those animals that needlessly suffered and died,
while all those in authority who could have acted,
did nothing tangible to help them.
And to all those at Heathrow Airport, who risked the hazards of infectious
disease and injury while tirelessly caring for the animals day and night to give them
a better chance of surviving their journeys.

This Revised Edition © 2016 John Brookland

All Photographs © 1985 John Brookland

Printed by Createspace

ISBN 13: 978-1519300164
10:1519300166

Original booklet printed with funding from the Animal Welfare Institute (AWI) & Humane Society of the United States (HSUS) on behalf of EIA & the authors and presented to the 5th. CITES Conference in Buenos Aires, Argentina 1985 by John Brookland and Nick Carter. This revised edition written and published by John Brookland (2016).

CONTENTS

Foreword by Sir Peter Scott, CBE, DSC   4

Authors Note   5

Background   5

Introduction   8

The Catching & Preparation of Live Specimens for Shipment   8

Mortality Caused by the Trade: Examples   11

Some Incidents of Injury, Damage to Health & Cruel Treatment   16

Mortality in Quarantine & Holding Following Transport   19

Wild Specimens Not Adapted to Captivity   19

Shipment of Immature Specimens   20

Species Vulnerable to Mortality During   21

The Effects of Stress, Debility and Disease on Mortalities   22

Importance of Animal Holding Facilities at Major Airports   30

City of London Animal Quarantine Station Heathrow   31

The UK Transit of Animals (General) Order, 1973   32

Avoidance of London Heathrow Airport   33

Standards of Inspection at Points of Export & Import   35

Traders in Wildlife   37

Diseases & Health Risks   38

The IATA Live Animals Regulations Manual   41

CITES Guidelines for Transport of Live Wild Animals   43

Practical Application of CITES Requirements   43

Repatriation of Specimens   44

Endangered Species in Transit   44

Addendum (2016)   45

Conclusions and Recommendations   46

Appendix

FOREWORD

I welcome this study of the commercial trade in live animals, although its findings are devastating. The Convention on International Trade in Endangered Species of Wild fauna and Flora stands foursquare for protection of animals in transit against damage to health and cruel treatment. Indeed, the text of the treaty repeats this provision in several different sections. But the photographs reproduced here and accompanied by first-hand reports show how disastrously these requirements, ratified by 87 nations, are being ignored.

Countries that export birds, primates and other animals need the facts and recommendations in this Study. No nation would willingly lose a substantial part of its wildlife heritage through the cruelty and death inflicted on the animals exported to make large profits for international animal dealers. But the middlemen in this business are reluctant to provide enough space or even adequate facilities for feeding and watering en-route because they grudge the relatively small cost of making proper provision for the animals. Airlines, too, must bear their share of the blame when they accept animals crated in such a way that they are likely to suffocate or die of thirst, or when they are exposed to extremes of temperature for lack of staff attention.

There are some encouraging signs that this appalling trade will be curtailed. For example, wild birds will no longer be imported for sale in New York when their Wild Bird Act comes into effect later this year. The new law arises from public concern for exotic birds suffering extreme privation and disease in commercial shipments. Mortality figures are staggering in many cases, and after arrival more deaths occur, while they are being held in quarantine. Some species of birds have been severely depleted in the wild through excesses of the pet trade. The gravity of the situation calls for urgent action by governments and organizations concerned for the humane treatment of animals and for their continued existence in the wild.

This booklet summarizes only part of a study undertaken by the authors, and uses excerpts from a more detailed report so that a wider group of readers can be made aware of the situation.

Sir Peter Scott, CBE, DSC.
Slimbridge,
Gloucester.
1985

AUTHORS NOTE

The reasons for revising and re-issuing this excerpted report are threefold. Firstly, to my knowledge, only snippets of the original 490 page report "The Preparation and Shipment of Live Fauna in International Trade Carried by Air" and only a handful of this accompanying booklet, which was distributed to most delegates at the fifth CITES Conference in Buenos Aires (1985), still exist. As one of the authors who put in years of research to produce it I hope this revision will be a permanent reminder and source of information.

The second is that at the time it caused quite a lot of consternation amongst all those connected with the transport of animals by air, receiving widespread publicity and was instrumental in galvanising the attention of delegates at the CITES Conference to the issue of cruelty and wasteful mortality of wildlife associated with the animal trade by air.

Thirdly it took four decades to get bans on the import of wild exotic birds into many countries such as the EU, while pro and anti-trade lobbyists argued over the misrepresentation of statistics and facts in order to either thwart or propose international legislation and now unfortunately history is repeating itself again in regard to the trade in reptiles. The same antagonists have been at it again for two decades discussing and arguing over the pros and cons of the trade while countless numbers of reptiles worldwide continue to suffer and die just like the birds before them.

A reminder of what happened with the bird trade might be timely, as it was always obvious to those that worked on the 'front line', that there is no way of avoiding widespread suffering and deaths amongst the mass numbers involved in the capture, shipment and holding of animals to supply the pet trade, whatever their species, and every effort should be made to curtail such trade where-ever and whenever possible.

BACKGROUND

Article III para 2(c), 4(b); Article IV para 29(c), 5(b) & 6 (b); Article V para (2b) & Article VIII specify that the Parties of CITES shall ensure "that all living specimens, during any period of transit, holding or shipment are properly cared for so as to minimise the risks *of injury, damage to health or cruel treatment*". It is therefore recognised internationally that the practical application of adequate animal welfare standards is mandatory for the effective conservation policy application of the CITES Convention.

At the fourth meeting of CITES, the Parties resolved that "for so long as the CITES Secretariat and Technical Committee agree, IATA Live Animal Regulations are generally deemed to meet CITES Guidelines in respect of air transport, and a continuing dialogue between CITES and IATA be developed including the suggestion of appropriate amendments to the IATA Live Animal Regulations".

While employed as an animal health inspector at the London Heathrow Airport Animal Quarantine Station (AQS) between 1977 and 1982 responsible for the care of the animals and the enforcement of disease and animal welfare regulations, I was appalled at the amount of suffering and death caused during transport by air to both wild and domestic animals and the apparent lack of concern by airlines, shippers and government agencies in combating it. I had also witnessed such incidents while associated with the RSPCA Airport Animal Hostel from the early 1970's.   I was also frustrated at a Government applied exemption enabling airlines and shippers to by-pass the Station and inspection of shipments as long as they were removed to onward flights or collected by the importer within four hours. This exposed a complete lack of understanding and interest in the welfare implications of this particular economic trade and resulted in Inspectors having to search cargo sheds for shipments with many not being examined for either disease or welfare regulation.

The high mortality, suffering and poor handling of animals being transported by air had been well documented for many decades and even as far back as 1927 the Zoological Society of London held a conference to discuss concerns over standards of shipment of animals by sea. Since the early 1950's, the Royal Society for the Prevention of Cruelty to Animals (RSPCA) had documented and publicised the suffering and death of animals in air transport witnessed through their airport animal facility at London, Heathrow, but had failed to improve conditions. In 1967 the International Council for Bird Preservation (ICPB) held a conference on the poor conditions of capture and transport of imported exotic birds, followed eight years later by two publications by the Royal Society for Protection of Birds (RSPB): 'All Heaven in a Rage' in 1975 and "Airborne Birds" in 1976 both researched and written by Tim Inskipp following painstaking research at the RSPCA Airport Animal Hostel.

Even though Tim Inskipps' reports revealed beyond doubt that IATA regulations were commonly ignored and not enforced and that bird mortality was high, there was little or no attempt to officially investigate and take action. Although most concern was aimed at birds, which constituted the bulk of those animals transported, it was common knowledge that all types of animals were suffering, but for several decades nothing was done to improve the situation.

In 1975 the airline industry's International Air Transport Association (IATA) published guidelines on the design and methods for transporting all types of animals by air. Although commendable, much of the information and advice was detrimental to the animals in practice and were drawn up without any clear evidence that the information provided was correct or beneficial. Not that this mattered as no one enforced the regulations and airlines continued to accept shipments as they had always historically done.

Over a period of 6 years I took a procession of prosecutions, under the UK Transit of Animals (General) Order 1973 welfare legislation (now the Welfare of Animals (Transport) Order, 2006) at Uxbridge Court against airlines for causing unnecessary suffering and using sub-standard containers. Some of these were ground-breaking as they included animals such as frogs and turtles which had never been treated as sentient animals that could suffer pain or distress, but again airlines dismissed these as collateral damage. As one airline representative said to me after being found guilty "you can carry on prosecuting us, but let's face it, the fine is just the cost of one tyre on an aircraft". In general airlines treated live animal shipments like any other freight and there appeared to be a mood of acceptance by all parties involved, including Government and veterinary officials that it was too big a challenge to tackle. Even when poor shipment practices and animal welfare issues were pointed out to Government veterinary officials in cargo sheds, they were not willing to get involved: their only interest being disease control rather than animal welfare.

It was with this background that I decided to try and do something to highlight the problem once and for all and along with a colleague Cheryl Hora, documented and photographed as many shipments as we could. We then decided to try and get financial backing to investigate what happened to these animals at the point of capture and export. As funding was not forthcoming we travelled to many of the major exporting countries at our own expense with accreditation from the IUCN and CITES, interviewing Government personnel, airline officials and animal traders. This resulted in a 490 page report entitled "The Preparation and Shipment of Wild Fauna in International Trade Carried by Air". This report was taken up by the U.K Environmental Investigation Agency (EIA), the U.S Animal Welfare Institute (AWI) and the Humane Society of the United States (HSUS) who funded further research and printed this report in 1985 to be presented to CITES and IATA at their 1985 Conference.

John Brookland
Essex, 2016

INTRODUCTION

This booklet is a summary of a 490-page study entitled 'The Preparation and Shipment of Wild Fauna in International Trade Carried by Air'. The four years' work for this study was undertaken solely on the initiative of the authors. The project was not funded by any organization, but was, however, endorsed by the Secretariat of the Convention on International Trade in Endangered Species (CITES) and the Wildlife Trade Monitoring Unit (WTMU) of the International Union for the Conservation of Nature (IUCN).

The terms of this study are defined in the Convention on International Trade in Endangered Species (CITES) in those clauses that specify:

- 'Management Authorities of the Parties shall be satisfied that any living specimen will be so prepared and shipped as to minimize the risk of injury, damage to health or cruel treatment;'
- 'that any living specimen will be so handled as to minimize the risk of injury, damage to health or cruel treatment;'
- 'a proposed recipient of a living specimen is suitably equipped to house and care for it.'

The study was researched during the period 1977-1983 from records of the City of London, Animal Quarantine Station and RSPCA Airport Hostel, London Heathrow Airport, during which time 1.5 million animals passed through these facilities. In 1982, 96% of all UK exotic bird imports were monitored in detail. In 1983 the authors visited many wildlife importing and exporting countries in Africa, India, S.E.Asia and USA, where over 60 individuals connected with all aspects of the trade were interviewed. During the period 1977-1982, the authors were employed in an official capacity at the AQS with responsibility for all aspects of welfare and UK import controls involved in the trade and transportation of animals by air.

This study shows that extremely unsuitable conditions still exist and also seeks to accurately define the conditions in which animals are transported, 13 years after supposed implementation of regulations by airlines to improve these conditions. Problem areas involving the daily enforcement of the IATA Live Animal Regulations and CITES requirements have been focused upon, and recommendations for improvements are suggested.

The trade is seen from the point of view of capture, preparation and shipment to eventual purchase and quarantine in consumer countries. When reviewed from this perspective, an enormous tragedy comes to light: wholesale wastage of wildlife in quantities hitherto unrealized.

The Catching & Preparation of Live Animals for Transport

Most mortality occurs during catching and preparation for shipment, and in quarantine or holding following transport by air. While airlines are responsible for accepting sub-standard shipments in violation of IATA Live Animals Regulations and CITES Guidelines, the evidence indicates that in practice their personnel rely

Red-masked Conures from Peru, overcrowded in crates, eagerly await food and water on arrival at London Heathrow Airport.

on traders acting in good faith. The facts regarding ante and post transportation mortality confirm the main responsibilities lie with the exporters, despite trader and trader association criticisms of IATA Live Animal Regulations, and the blaming of airlines for mortalities.

Conditions in which wild fauna are kept prior to export or sale vary considerably between different traders and also from country to country. At virtually all premises visited by the authors, conditions were unsatisfactory in terms of preparation for shipment.

Very few, if any wildlife traders organize their own catching expeditions, but for economic reasons rely on local trappers. The trappers, often farmers, lack the expertise, knowledge or facilities to care for the animals adequately. Many specimens die or are injured during capture. They may then be held for long periods awaiting collection by the exporter's representative, or may be transported under inhumane or over-crowded conditions to central collection points. From there, they are transported long distances to exporter's premises near the point of export. The condition of the animals is habitually very poor on arrival and according to one exporter mortality up to this point can be as high as 50% or more.

Depending on the exporter, the animals may be shipped immediately or kept for an acclimatization period. Birds are often kept in reception aviaries where those in relatively sound condition with reasonable plumage are gradually transferred to

Baby terrapins shipped from the USA, 200 per container in cheap cardboard boxes resulting in several incidents when boxes were crushed causing heavy mortality.

holding pens. Those birds that are dying, weak or mutilated are left to either die or recover. Veterinary attention is normally out of the question particularly in the case of commoner species such as small finches, so popular in the pet trade. At one premises visited by the authors, over 20,000 birds were seen of which at least 20% had no chance of survival. At another, species were seen mixed together in overcrowded conditions, in cages that had not been cleaned for days, causing considerable fighting and mortality.

Primates suffer a similar fate. One primate exporter stated that he shipped them within 24-48 hours of receiving them from the trapper. This removed the need to care for them and reduced risks of illness and disease occurring on his premises which might delay export. It was preferable to have such problems occur at the destinations where veterinary attention could be provided in quarantine, but this obviously increased the risk of suffering and death being caused during transport. The shipment of essentially unexamined primates which may, or may not, be suffering from illness or disease clearly is risky, both for them, other animals and to humans coming into contact with them during transit and on arrival in quarantine. Mortality amongst primates undergoing 90 day quarantine in the USA has been as much as 50% or more. An Indonesian trader once stated that 60-70% of the macaques trapped in Indonesia died prior to shipment. Whether this is an over estimate or not, the mortality is high due to the methods of capture and holding.

Those animals lucky enough to survive to the point of shipment then face long journeys by air, mostly under sub-standard conditions. In the case of birds, UK

Doves shipped in cardboard boxes heading for research with no thought given or understanding of how they might be loaded in the aircraft hold. These boxes were easily crushed and had no access doors or food or water facilities if delayed.

and USA statistics show that between 3.8 to 4.2% of the total birds shipped die during transport and many more arrive in poor condition. On arrival at their destinations, their suffering of the continues when they are often confined in overcrowded and unhygienic conditions where the stresses of their recent past become too much for them.

On many occasions shipments are refused entry due to health or documentation problems and are either destroyed or are forced to face further transport to a different country of import. Deaths in quarantine in the UK and USA, including destruction, account for a further 20% or more mortality in birds and 50% in primates. Eventually the animals arrive at laboratories, zoos and as pets where the short lifespan of many species and the demand for replacements causes the trade to continue.

Examples of Mortality Caused in the Trade.

Standards of crating and holding prior to shipment and the mortality caused, varies from country to country. This study has shown that most countries have a poor record in this respect and among them are Senegal, Tanzania and Ethiopia which are used here to illustrate the degree of mortality that is inflicted on wild specimens.

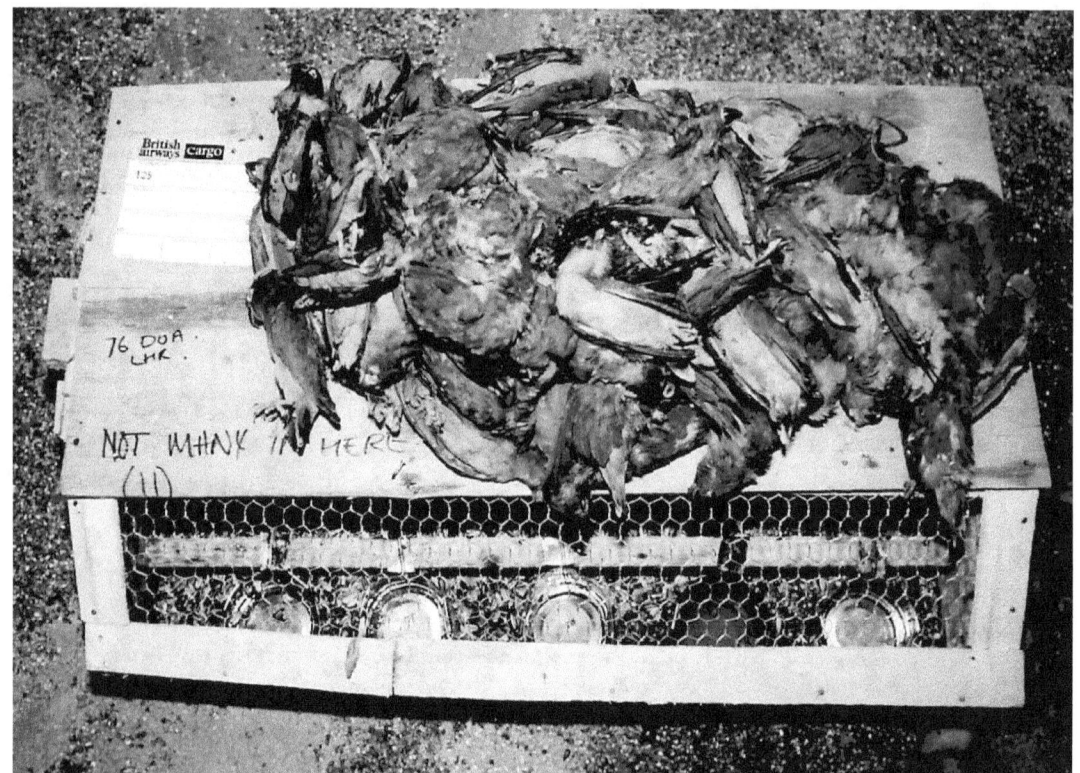

One box of a shipment of 2,000 lovebirds from Tanzania packed 80-90 per crate with inadequate ventilation and water facilities. 400 (20%) were dead on arrival at London Heathrow. In this particular box only 11 survived out of 87 crammed inside. (1982)

Senegal is among the largest existing exporters of wild birds supplying a substantial proportion of the international market with small seed-eating species so popular as pets. Annual exports averaged 1,204,000 birds during the period 1977-1981, that's just over 6 million in five years. Senegal exported birds to over twenty countries in 1981 of which the USA and France were the largest importers.

Shipments imported into the UK regularly arrived in poor condition due to a combination of overcrowding, lack of adequate food and water and the shipment of species unable to endure the rigors and stresses of transport. Birds were often trampled with numbers blinded by pecking. Some drowned in water pots, evidently at or near the time they began their journey since all the pots were usually empty on arrival. Simple remedies like putting soft wood floats in the pots would have saved thousands of lives. Only seed husks usually remained, indicating food, like water, had been consumed early on.

Of 83,420 birds imported into the UK in 1982 from Senegal, 3,219 (3.9%) died during transit by air with additional losses in quarantine. Taking UK mortality figures during transport by air as a sample average over 45,000 birds are likely to have died in transit from Senegal during 1981. A safe conservative estimate of post travel mortalities is 200,000 or 20% of the stated exports if UK and USA quarantine and transit mortalities are considered average.

Taking capture, post-capture, travel and holding for export mortalities as stated to Bruggers (Export of Cage Birds from Senegal, IUCN Bulletin Vol. IV, No2, July

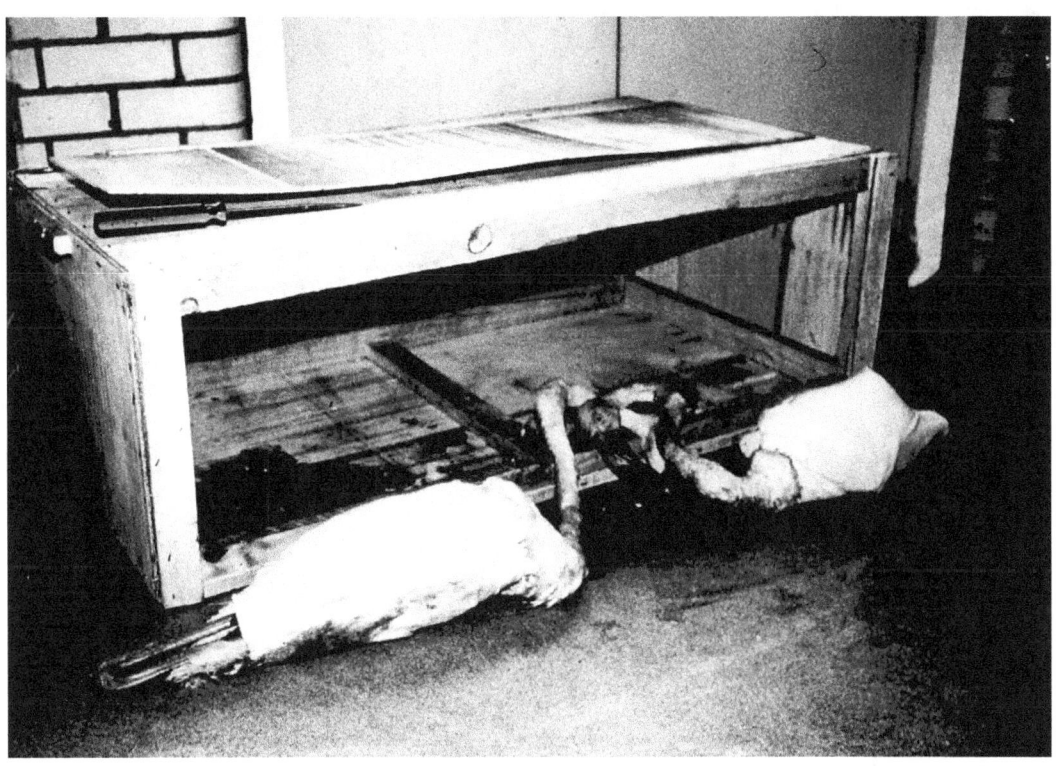

Part of a shipment of 20 Flamingos in transit from Tanzania of which 3 were dead on arrival at London, Heathrow and the remainder were suffering from multiple wounds to wings and legs and unable to stand due to blood circulation loss having been confined in tight non-elastic strapping. This was one species unsuitable for trade as there was really no appropriate method to transport them safely.

1982), in conjunction with the mortality findings discussed in this report, the resultant wastage is as follows:

During capture:	40% - 50%
Post-capture transport:	2% - 3%
Awaiting sale and shipment:	12% - 16%
Air Transport:	3.8% – 3.8%
Post-Transit (UK):	16% - 16%
Mortality range	73.8% - 88.8%

Tanzania which mainly exports lovebirds and small seed-eating species was found to have one of the worst records for standards of shipment, which regularly arrived in the UK in appallingly over-crowded conditions in sub-standard crates. Up to 90 lovebirds were often crammed into crates with hardly room to move and unable to access any water that might have been provided. In transit mortalities of 20% or more were common. In an incident involving flamingos, the birds arrived with their legs and wings strapped tightly in non-elastic cloth causing swollen joints, bleeding wounds and some deaths.

The crate on the left is typical of those seen from Ethiopian primate shippers. Each compartment contained two large baboons (see below) which were hardly able to move. No food or water was provided. For onward carriage the author insisted on new crates, the one on the right being of minimum size for one animal per compartment as required by IATA Regulations. The airline continued to accept such shipments regardless of countless warnings. (1982)

Confused and dejected young baboons receiving care before being crated for onward travel.

Many pregnant females gave birth or aborted their young during the stress of transport.

In 1982, UK imports from Tanzania numbered 13,682 of which 729 (5.4%) were dead on arrival with many more in a poor state. Of 10,521 transhipped through Heathrow for other countries, 874 (8.3%) were dead on arrival at Heathrow. If these figures are related to those of Senegal, it is probable that losses during capture, internal transport and holding prior to export are higher. The overall wastage of life may be in the order of 80-90%.

Considerable problems were experienced with Baboon and Vervet monkey shipments arriving from Ethiopia. The baboons were packed individually or in pairs in partitioned crates of sub-standard wood. Despite complaints to the airline involved and the continual problems caused by these non-IATA regulation crates which were too small and lacked food and water facilities, the same design containers were continually used. Baboons were literally wedged in the compartments unable to sit upright and sadly, on occasions, found sitting on the body of their companion. The poor construction often resulted in them escaping into the holds of aircraft. Vervets were usually transported individually in partitioned crates again without food or water facilities. They were generally in poor bodily condition with wounds, diarrhoea and bronchial infections plus coughing and sneezing.

Although at Heathrow the mortality rate was low, the incidence of suffering was great. Many pregnant females gave birth to still born young or aborted. There is evidence that the poor standards of preparation and shipment resulted in high post-transit mortality. US import and quarantine statistics show that between January

1978 and September 1979, of 970 Vervet monkeys imports from Ethiopia, 269 (27.2%) arrived dead with a further 209 (21.5%) dying during the first 90 days: a total death toll of 49.2%. Among baboons the mortality was 12.9% of the total imports.

The common factors to the foregoing cases and borne out by the accompanying photographs are:

1. the evident sole concern of the traders with reducing container sizes to economise on freight charges and manifest unconcern for the living specimens;
2. the acceptance by airlines of improperly crated live specimens despite obvious unsuitability apparent even to persons unfamiliar with animals;
3. neglect to use their own IATA Live Animals regulations as the standard;
4. inefficiency of enforcement agencies at exporting inspection points.

Mortality During Quarantine and Holding Following Transport

Mortalities during quarantine and holding are as significant as catching and transport factors. There is some similarity between the patterns of bird and primate deaths in quarantine. The following table illustrates the in-transit and quarantine deaths of birds imported into the UK and USA:

	UK Bird Imports 1980-1982	US Bird Imports 1976-1983	Average
Total Birds imported:	712,398	4,786,621	
In-Transit Deaths:	26,929	200,281	
Percentage:	3.8%	4.2%	4.1%
Died During Quarantine:	77,003	817,445	
Percentage:	11.2%	17.8%	16.9%,

Figures published in Traffic (USA), Vol.3, 1981 show that of 42,464 primates of over 12 species imported into the country between January 1978 and September 1979 from 13 countries, 1,743 (4.1%) were dead on arrival and 4,754 (11.7%) died in quarantine.

Statistics show that the majority of deaths occur in the first few weeks following arrival. The causes for the mortality reflect the consequences of prolonged stress during transport – with the resultant severe debility, liability to sickness and the incapacity to recover and adapt – and the poor standards of preparation and shipment. Many deaths may be attributed to sub-standard quarantine conditions.

There have been examples in the UK of high mortality in quarantine caused by inadequate conditions and management. One such example involved a consignment of 201 birds of 12 species including mynah birds, cockatoos, lorikeets, white-eyes, fruit-suckers and thrushes. The birds had only suffered 3 deaths during transit and were crated in reasonably good conditions. During quarantine the consignment suffered 95 deaths. Birds began to die soon after arrival and the veterinary surgeon supervising the premises was consulted. Autopsy showed that many had died of starvation, later found to be due to wrong feeding. Obviously the ignorance of the proprietor of the premises and the veterinary surgeon lacking the requisite knowledge to rectify the situation were culpable.

8 out of 10 giant river otters died during transport on an Air Canada flight and the surviving two were severely traumatised and distressed. The otters were consigned in two individually partitioned crates with a narrow opening for ventilation which had needlessly been covered with peg board, almost cutting off all ventilation. It was also alleged that the crates were covered in other freight in the hold. The veterinary surgeon called in to examine the shipment stated: "*The high mortality rate was entirely due to poor packaging. The ventilation was totally inadequate due to the addition of pegboard over the mesh thereby reducing the airflow, complicated by solid partitions between the animals and wood shavings being pushed up against the ventilation holes. There was evidence of violent efforts to escape by the unfortunate animals and a considerable amount of blood splashed around causing very considerable suffering before their untimely deaths*". Air Canada fined £1,200 plus £75 costs (1980).

Small specialist importers may be able to provide adequate facilities to house animals adequately, and even give individual attention, but large importers, who may handle many thousands at one time, find it uneconomical or even impractical to offer proper care. Therefore, birds are often kept in poor conditions, which in many cases, leads to high mortality. Similar conditions also occur in the USA and elsewhere.

Most importing countries do not require prospective importers to provide evidence of their knowledge, experience or competence in caring for captive live animals. Authorities also appear not to insist on suitable welfare conditions in quarantine or be able to provide veterinary inspectors with the specialized knowledge or experience to supervise quarantine premises.

Ten Howler monkeys and 20 Capuchin monkeys in unsuitable containers from Paraguay via Lima and Paris to London. Estimated journey time with delays was 84 hours. The boxes had no facilities for food or water, slatted floors or doors. The above box measured 8.5 inches high (21.5 cm) and was severely overcrowded containing ten monkeys which when sitting comfortably measured 14 inches (35.5 cm) high. The monkeys were literally soaked with urine, faeces and rotten banana and showed signs of stiffness in their limbs having been almost unable to move. The capuchin monkeys suffered similar deprivation and suffered two deaths during transit. All ten Howlers died in quarantine soon after arrival. In the veterinary surgeons opinion they were *"caused a great deal of suffering due to totally unsuitable containers and severe over-crowding"*. Air France was fined £1,700 for causing unnecessary suffering.

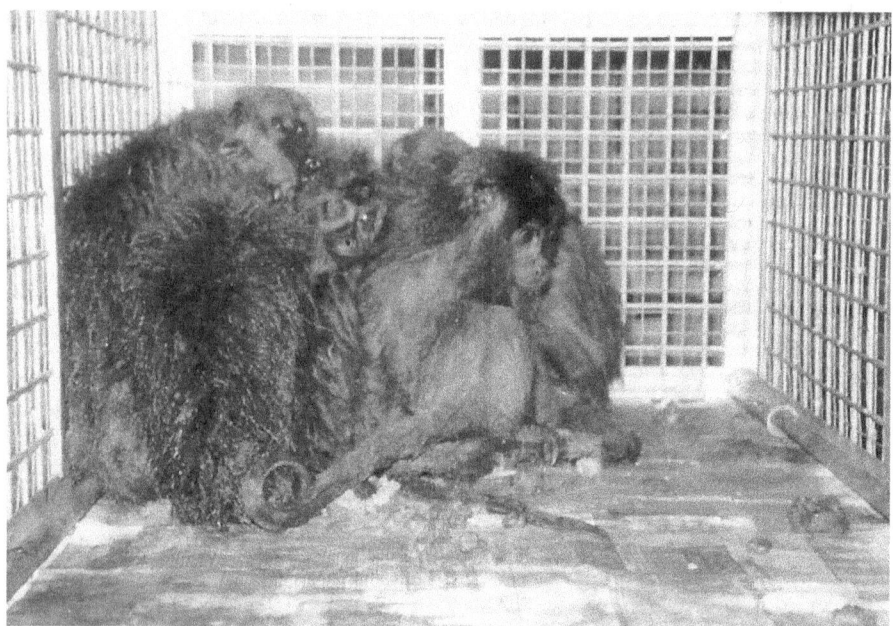

Some of the traumatised Howler monkeys soon after release.

Observations on Some Causes of Mortality in Relation to Preparation and Shipment

Numerous factors govern mortality rates among animals in international trade. The following 'mortality tree' illustrates the main causes:

Poor crating	}	**Overcrowding, Injury**	} **High Mortality**
Poor Health, Disease	}	**Dehydration, Starvation**	
Lack of Food & Water	}	**Dirt, Suffocation**	
Delays In Transit	}	**Fright, Stress**	
Poor Stowage in Aircraft	}	**Varying temperature**	
Immaturity	}		

Five main problem areas are identifiable:

    i.   shipment of wild specimens not adapted to captivity, unprepared for transport and so highly vulnerable to stress and mortality;

    ii.   shipment of immature, pregnant and species requiring special treatment making them unsuitable species for transport;

    iii.   capture and holding induces stress or shock due to intemperate handling resulting in poor health and disease susceptibility making them unfit for travel;

    iv.   poor crating; mixing species; overcrowding; lack of food and water; privacy;

    v.   poor stowage in aircraft holds and cargo sheds; delays; accidents.

The authors' experience and observations in this study indicate responsibility for problems (i) to (iv) lie with traders and items under (v) concern airlines.

Wild Specimens Not Adapted to Captivity

Comparison between wild caught and captive bred birds shipped by air highlights the unsuitability of shipping specimens un-acclimatized to human contact and captivity and therefore unprepared for shipment.

Most, if not all birds exported from Taiwan and Czechoslovakia are captive bred and include cockatiels, lovebirds and white java sparrows. Shipments from these countries, imported to the UK, were found to suffer only 0.5% mortality during transit compared with 3.9% of wild caught birds from Senegal and 5.4% from Tanzania.

Shipments from Taiwan and Czechoslovakia were not adequately crated in terms of IATA Live Animals Regulations, but the birds, considering the long flight time from Taiwan, appeared to withstand the conditions better as the figures attest. These birds seemed to tolerate and be less stressed as a result of being crowded into crates, having been used to such an environment and also close and frequent interaction with their human carers. None were suffering the post capture and transit stress readily observable in the behaviour of wild caught birds.

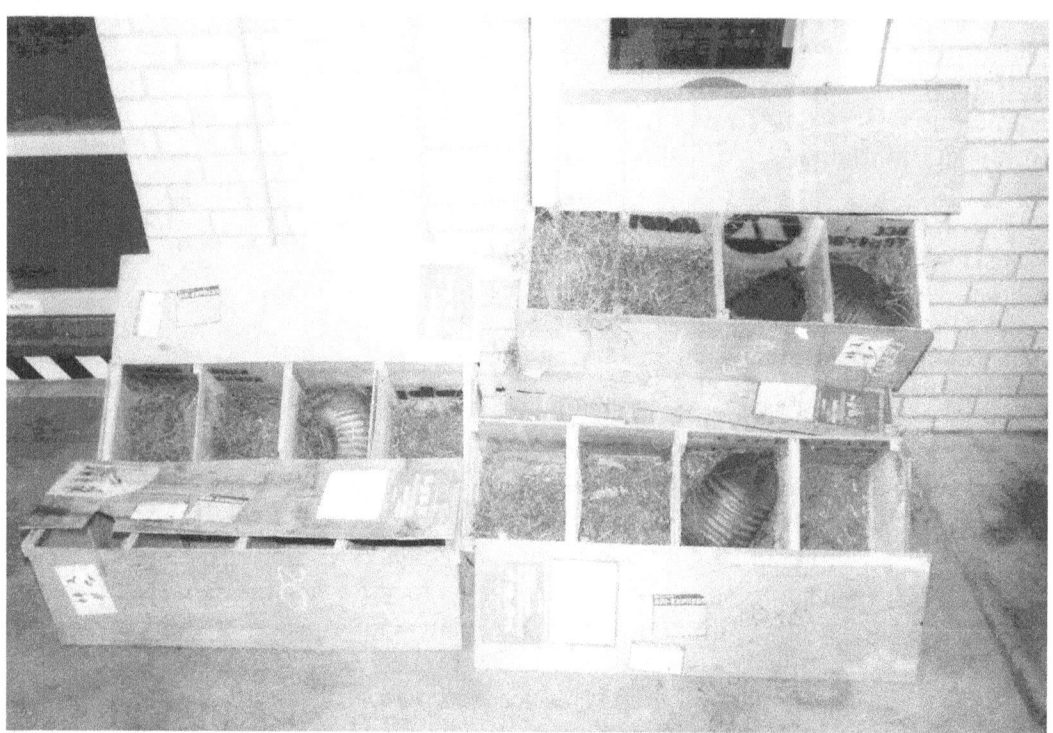

These armadillos were shipped from Miami to London in thin poorly constructed plywood crates with insufficient ventilation. Three of the armadillos were loose in the aircraft hold and and had to be captured by AQS staff causing long delays to the aircraft. Four of the larger animals were found dead with their heads wedged in the corners as can be seen above. In the examining veterinary surgeon's opinion: *"The construction and packaging of these containers was such as to cause unnecessary suffering, both due to extremely poor ventilation aggravated by very densely packed bedding material and restricted space. The strength of the containers was inadequate bearing in mind that they are powerful digging animals"*. The US National Airlines ceased operation before the case could be heard.

Shipment of Immature Specimens

Usually it is parrots, macaws and mynah birds which are shipped as "gapers" i.e. birds requiring hand-feeding. The younger the birds, the easier, according to traders, it is to hand tame them and secure a higher price. If no delays occur during transit, shippers usually escape without high mortality. Clearly, there is a great risk factor here and the trade does not "minimize risk of injury, damage to health or cruel treatment". And no rational person may expect airline personnel to hand feed substantial numbers of unfledged birds in the event of delays: which unfortunately for many reasons are common.

A shipment of 384 Amazon parrots, too young to identify accurately, and dependent on hand-feeding, were delayed at Heathrow destined for the USA. Over 150 (39%) died by the time they reached Chicago.

Baby 'gaper' parrots requiring regular hand-feeding and shipped without any thought to their chances of survival should a delay occur or being exposed to inclement climate conditions.

Species Vulnerable to Mortality During Transport & Holding

Certain families of birds, and some species of families, travel badly following capture and crating. The mortality rates of such species are sufficiently high to suggest that they are constitutionally incapable of being prepared and shipped so as to minimize the risk of injury, damage to health or cruel treatment. The question is complicated by poor crating standards and inadequate care. Some species may have a higher survival rate if suitably prepared and shipped, whereas others seem likely to suffer and eventually die no matter how carefully treated. The condition in which specimens arrive clearly influences their survival rates in quarantine.

The authors have compiled a list of the species, found by the study, to regularly suffer high mortality during transport and quarantine. The list includes many of the popular seed-eating species imported as pets, such as the fire-finch, cordon bleu and green singing finch.

The continued shipment of species with known poor survival rates is among the major problems of shipping birds by air. Discrimination with respect to species in need of particular attention is essential. If this is impractical in present conditions consideration should be given to preventing trade in species most vulnerable to trade-induced mortality. By such means overall mortality rates of air transported birds may be notably decreased.

Some of the 25 crates containing hundreds of live frogs. The animals were piled on top of each other with legs and arms protruding through slats causing multiple deaths and injuries. Jugoslovenski Aerotransport (JAT) was fined £500 for using improper crates and causing unnecessary suffering.

Piles of dead Lovebirds the result of overcrowding and lack of adequate ventilation.

The Effects of Stress, Debility and Disease on Mortalities

Major stresses are caused by the capture, confinement and transport of wild specimens in international trade. These cumulative stresses cause debility and increased susceptibility to diseases which may manifest themselves only during air transport or at post transit holding facilities. The general conditions of international trade significantly increase the opportunities for the development and spread of animal diseases and zoonosis.

Animals may, after capture, pass through the hands of a number of middlemen before reaching the exporters. In this period they are commonly kept in unhygienic, overcrowded conditions, sustained with food by persons whose priorities are with commerce rather than with proper preparations for shipment to foreign countries.

The shipment of debilitated and/or diseased specimens is common. Experience at Heathrow Airport suggests that health certificates are usually meaningless in respect of animals suffering from a range of injurious diseases to which the stresses of capture and holding have made them vulnerable. Such diseases often may be dormant and prior to shipment it may be difficult, if not impossible, for veterinary surgeons to perceive or diagnose sickness by visual examination. Many countries lack facilities to make thorough tests possible.

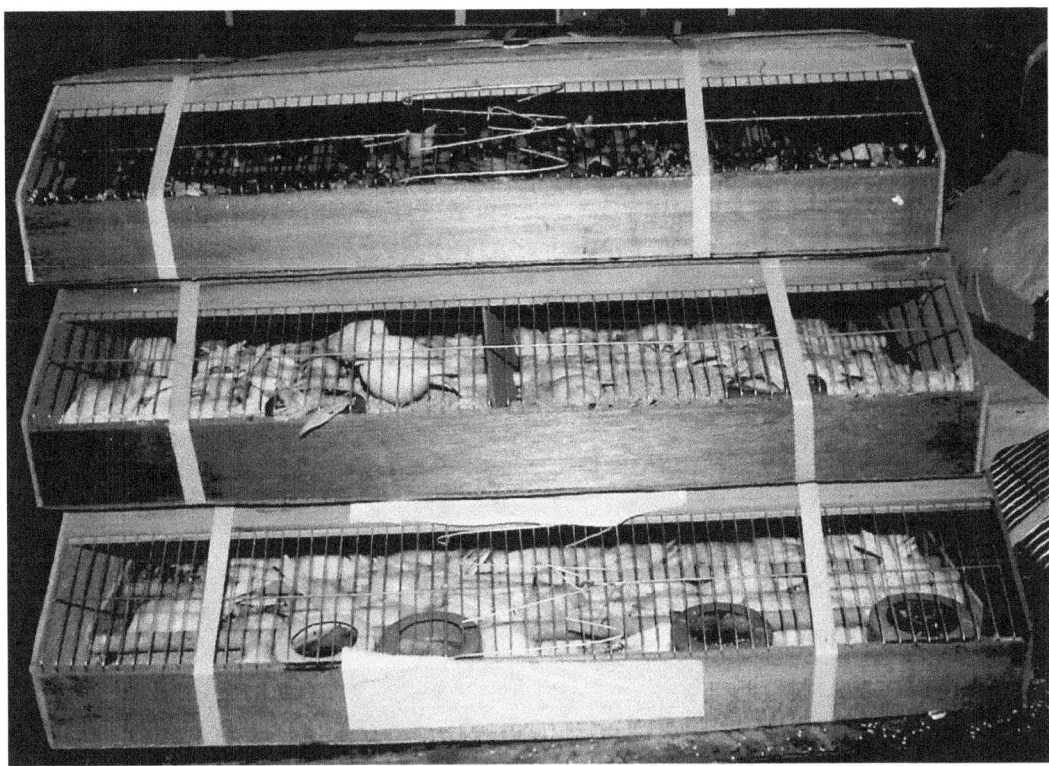

Dead birds litter the floors of crates awaiting removal by Heathrow animal facility staff while two lone survivors stand amid the carnage.

Overcrowding

Wild specimens are unadapted to confinement, human proximity and handling, and many are non-gregarious species. The stress factor among wild species of birds and animals in transport renders comparisons with domestic species and humans inadmissible. From experience at Heathrow Airport it may be stated categorically that overcrowding is a major problem

Overcrowding affects:
  i.   the amount of food and water available for each bird;
  ii. the air and perching space available and the associated build-up of body heat within the crates;
  iii. the degree of stress imposed on the birds;
  iv. air pollution due to droppings.

Overcrowding varies from country to country and from shipper to shipper within the same country. Thailand, Tanzania and Senegal have poor records in this respect. Taiwan also has a poor record, although as mentioned earlier, the mainly captive bred birds appear to withstand the conditions much better unless ventilation is restricted when loaded into aircraft holds, which has resulted in heavy mortality.

It is relevant to compare sample shipments of birds from two Senegal dealers which arrived at Heathrow Airport within 24 hours of each other:

Table 1: Sample Shipments of Birds from Two Senegal Dealers to Illustrate Effects of Overcrowding:

	Shipment A	Shipment B
No. of Crates:	25	30
No. Of Birds:	4,850	3,780
Av. Birds per crate:	194	126
Size of crates:	24in.L x 18in. x 8in.H (60cm x 45cm x 20cm)	23in.L x 19in. x 8in.H (57.5cm x 47.5cm x 20cm)
No of water pots/crate:	4	4
No. of Perches:	5	5

Species	No.	DOA*	%	No.	DOA*	%
Siverbill:	450	32	7.1	190	-	-
Green Singing Finch:	400	93	23.2	750	14	1.8
Cordon Bleu:	600	90	15.0	375	5	1.3
Cuthroat:	600	19	3.1	450	3	0.6
Red-ear Waxbill:	800	20	2.5	375	7	1.8
Orange-cheek Waxbill:	800	6	0.7	920	6	0.6
Golden-breast Waxbill:	600	29	4.8	150	1	0.6
Lavender Finch:	200	11	5.5	100	-	-
Fire-Finch:	400	263	65.7	-	-	-
Golden Song Sparrow:				70	3	4.2
Aurora Finch:				200	7	3.5
Bronze-wing Mannikin:				200	-	-
Totals:	4,850	563	11.6 (av.)	3,780	46	1.2
(av.)						

*Dead on arrival: The birds in Shipment A were excessively overcrowded; many birds had drowned in water pots. Although other factors may have influenced the mortality in Shipment A there was no evidence of this. Higher mortality was always experienced in overcrowded crates.

Poor Crating

The incidence of poor crating is common and causes a great deal of unnecessary suffering and mortality. Each shipper has his own interpretation as to how crates should be constructed. Local usages over many years have habituated airlines to accepting them and with no obvious feed-back from transiting or importing points of any problems; there is no requirement to query their design. With little worldwide enforcement of adequate crating standards and no real agreement over whether the recommended designs are suitable, there is never any improvement in the situation as the mortality rates show.

It was common practice at Heathrow, particularly with primate shipments destined for research, to release the animals from woefully inadequate crates that were often half the required dimensions under IATA and insist on new IATA recommended crates before allowing onward shipment. Remarkably it is also common for pet dogs and cats to also be accepted for shipment in totally inadequately sized and designed containers highlighting the total disregard of IATA regulations across the board. Experience suggests that importers rarely question the

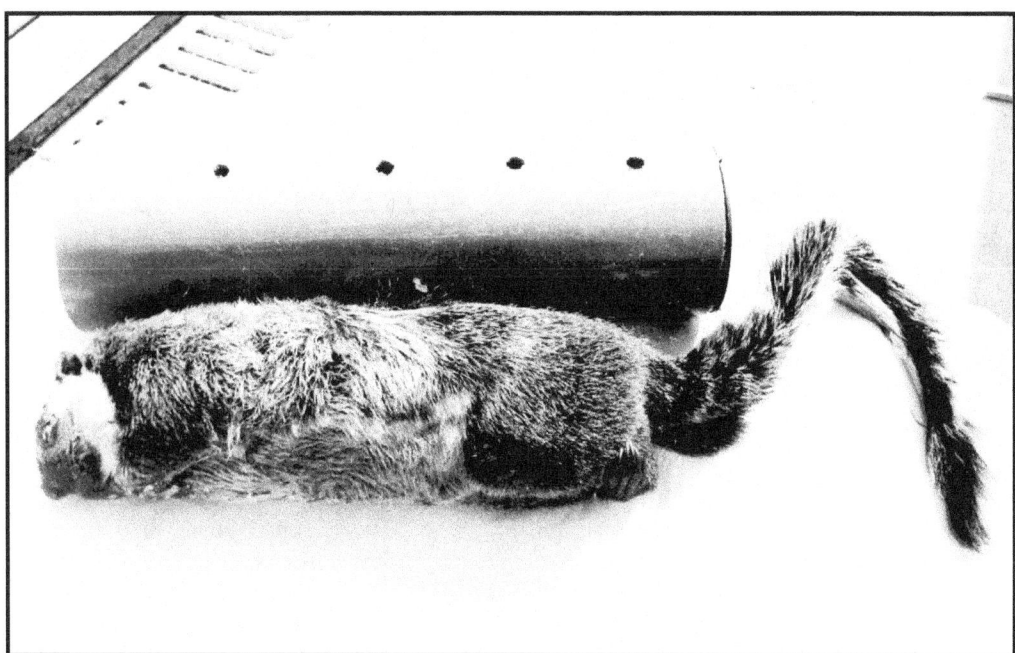

Ten Giant Squirrels from Indonesia were literally wedged into plastic drainage pipes, enclosed with tin ends and then stacked into a wooden crate without adequate ventilation. The squirrels were unable to move and were caused considerable suffering. Amazingly only two died, but the survivors were in a very poor condition and several if not all probably died later. This was one of the worst incidents of senseless and poor crating seen at Heathrow between 1977-1982.

causes of high mortality accepting it as collateral losses for which they can replace lost birds by securing credit from the exporter. The airlines warn shippers that they can accept no responsibility for mortalities in transit: commercially airlines are unaffected by them.

Table 2: A Comparison between Squirrel monkey shipments from Bolivia and Guyana showing effects of overcrowding & delay (1979)

Country of Origin:	Bolivia	Guyana
Routing:	Santa Cruz-Lima-Madrid -London-Japan	Georgetown-London-Japan
Estimated Transit Time:	72 hours (to London)	18 hours
Condition of monkeys:	Poor-emaciated-open Wounds	Generally good
Size of crate:	39in. x 20 x 12H (99cm x 50 x 30)	24in. x 22 x 28H (61cm x 56 x 71)
Construction:	Wooden-no door one water tin-wire grills all four sides-no seclusion difficult to access.	Wooden-similar to IATA with resting shelf. Door and and water pot, but difficult to access.
Monkeys per crate:	30	15
Cubic inches per monkey:	312 (5059 cu.cms)	985.6 (16,169 cu cms)
Food:	Banana – mostly rotten	Banana
Water:	Empty	Empty
No shipped:	935	507
Mortality at London:	71	4
Percentage:	7.6	0.8

Food and water
Considerable suffering and mortality is caused through lack of water. In particular birds become dehydrated very quickly and it is routine to see them clustered around empty water pots when they arrive at Heathrow, even after a short flight. Dead birds in water pots are a common sight. Any water that might be initially present is spilled through rough handling during loading and unloading. Birds either fall into or are pushed into pots and drown while awaiting shipment, especially if they are over-crowded or fly about the crate in panic. Very few crates have the right amount of water pots to cater for the number of birds, many are inaccessible for replenishment at transit stops and virtually none have 'floats' of soft wood to prevent drowning. In many primate crates, the restricted space does not allow for the provision of water or food pots.

Confined birds generate incredible amounts of heat causing excess thirst and an abnormal amount of water is taken. In most bird, primate and mammal crates, food is scattered on the floor which results in soiling from urine, and faeces. Lack of easily accessed doors makes feeding during transit difficult and in many cases impossible unless suitable facilities are available where crates can be opened. It was common practice at Heathrow to open and release animals from crates principally during long stopovers in order to be able to feed and water them and also give them

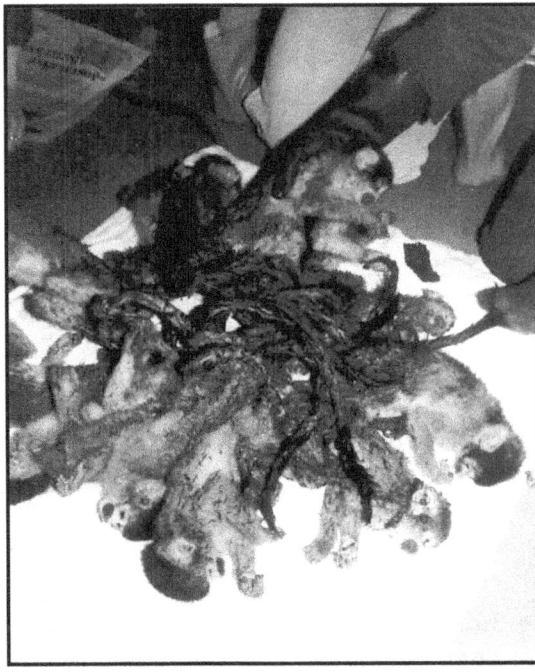

These 15 Squirrel Monkeys, part of a shipment of 29 in one crate were shipped from Bolivia to Japan via Lima, Madrid and London. On arrival at Heathrow, the monkeys were in a distressed state with a powerful smell of rotting banana and faeces emanating from the crate. When opened 14 monkeys were released, but the others were terrified, distressed and struggling, but appeared 'stuck' to the wire mesh floor. Staff were unable to extricate them so a veterinary surgeon was called, who anaesthetised them. It was discovered that due to overcrowding and the constant movement of the animals, their tails had become irreversibly 'tied' together. It took 30 minutes to untangle their tails and three were found dead on the bottom of the pile. Iberia Airlines was fined £400 for causing unnecessary suffering.

some relaxation. In most cases this was against the wishes of the exporter. There is nothing more pathetic than to see primates pushing their hands and arms through mesh begging for food and water or birds expectantly crowded round pots. It is important that every effort be made to feed and water at every opportunity.

Poor Stowage in Aircraft Holds

Instances of suffering and heavy mortality among animals and birds in international trade have been publicised in the press over the years and although such incidents are more the exception than the rule, the results are normally caused by poor stowage in the hold of the aircraft, delays due to technical faults, failure in heating and ventilation systems or bad weather or a combination of all.

It appears endemic in the attitude of airline personnel to treat live animals as normal freight, predominantly at points of origin, but also at major airports like Heathrow, without giving any consideration to the need of stable loading with sufficient air flow and heating. This is mainly due to lack of training and supervision. The authors have witnessed such poor stowage on many occasions when called by airline staff to attend aircraft following reports of loose animals in the hold or worries over disease.

Experience has shown at Heathrow that high mortality results when airlines are forced to use poor stowage methods when attempting to load and ship large consignments on one flight. This is principally the case with shipments destined for the USA which often number 100 containers of birds or more. One such incident in 1981, involved 8,000 birds in 87 crates which suffered 1,200 (19%) dead on arrival at Heathrow in transit to the USA. Mortalities were caused by a combination of suffocation, overheating and dehydration due to a massive build-up of heat in the crates when they were wrongly stacked blocking most of the ventilation. The sheer volume of such shipments in some cases makes it impossible for airline personnel to load them properly. For this, airlines are clearly at fault and a solution may be to restrict the volume accepted to what each aircraft hold is able to carry in a humane way.

Accidents

Some mortality is caused through technical faults which develop in flight. Clearly, these cannot be anticipated and the incidence is low. One such incident involved 199 birds in three crates of which 101 (50.7%) froze to death when the heating system failed. The floors of the crate were covered in ice and the carcasses were frozen solid. It was remarkable so many survived. The highest mortality was suffered by 76 kingfishers of which 65 (85.5%) died as these were in the bottom crate nearest the floor. The top crate suffered the fewest.

Delays during Transit

Delays during transit at airports with no facilities for the care of live shipments are a long standing problem. Few airports around the world have such amenities; those without them generally appear to be able to care for domestic dogs, cats and other pets, but are unequipped to handle delayed wildlife consignments. Problems occur with most frequency at European airports which handle larger volumes of live

Even though these birds were in crates supplied with ventilation on two sides, water pots and perches, they still suffered high mortality due to being stacked on the floor of the aircraft hold and covered and surrounded by other freight. Airline loaders need to be aware and trained how to handle live animal shipments.

Of 199 birds, mainly beautiful kingfishers, 101 (50.7%) died when the cargo hold heating system failed. Nearly all the dead were in the bottom crate on the floor of the hold. They froze to death and their carcasses were still frozen four hours after arrival. Had they been stowed above floor height more might have survived.

The all too common and distressing job of removing dead birds, which also poses a health risk to staff attending to such animals.

fauna. The immediate attention essential to the survival of specimens is often impractical, since most crates have no easily accessible or adequate food and water pots. In March 1981, three crates destined for the UK containing 146 mixed species of birds were delayed 24 hours at Paris airport due to bad weather conditions. The crates were not designed to facilitate easy watering or feeding. The birds appeared to have received no attention. Of eight Cock of the Rocks shipped, six were dead on arrival; of 50 hummingbirds 28 were dead; and of 24 tanagers, 4 were dead. The remaining birds were in very poor condition and also sustained mortalities.

In another incident on 7 July 1981, 12,000 assorted waxbills in 63 containers destined for Detroit in USA were delayed at Paris airport due to an industrial dispute. On arrival at Heathrow almost 1,000 were dead.

Such incidents highlight both the need for animal holding facilities at major airports and the use of containers so designed that watering and feeding can be carried out easily. Most importers and exporters do not appreciate their shipments being "tampered" with or the costs involved in looking after them, seemingly content to see them suffer or die in such incidents.

Importance of Animal Holding facilities at Major Airports

There is an important, if not indispensable, need for adequate facilities for handling live fauna in international trade at air and sea ports if human and animal health and welfare is to be protected from the consequences of malpractice and/or errors that commonly occur in this trade. Such amenities are few and far between with only a few airports such as Copenhagen, Schipol airport, Amsterdam and Frankfurt apart from Heathrow providing such services. Facilities are essential to the application of the Convention, and IATA Live Animal Regulations through national legislation and enforcement. Developed States with such facilities could supplement controls in others that cannot afford them

The advantages are in:
  i.   ensuring the health and welfare of animals during export, import and in transit in both human and animal interests;
  ii.   ensuring CITES provisions and IATA Regulations are applied in practice;
  iii. the accurate identification of species and numbers of specimens actually in trade to ensure the paper reality of permits and licences conforms with physical reality in the interests of endangered species legislation;
  iv.   accommodating delayed or seized shipments in proper conditions;
  v.   providing Customs and other enforcement agencies with the advice and co-operation necessary for effective enforcement;
  vi.   providing airline personnel with practical specialist assistance where necessary, as well as co-operative advisory and education services.

City of London Animal Quarantine Station (AQS), London Heathrow Airport

The AQS and its predecessor the RSPCA Animal Hostel have shown the value of an animal holding facility at a major airport in regulating and improving standards of shipment.

The Station was built at a cost of £750,000 and opened in 1977. It employs four Management/Animal Health Inspectors, office staff and fourteen animal attendants providing a 24 hour service for the care of all types of animals being imported, exported or in transit and the enforcement of legislation on behalf of the Ministry of Agriculture, Fisheries and Food. In 1982, the Station handled 450,000 animals and examined many more in cargo sheds and aircraft holds.

It is divided into two sections, one for export and import species not under quarantine controls, and one for those that are. Strict hygiene is enforced with disinfectant foot baths, protective clothing and special suits for dealing with diseased shipments. It has facilities for housing most species including isolation quarters, a surgery and an incinerator plus a large fully equipped vehicle for emergencies such as animals loose in aircraft holds or on the airport grounds, collection of unsafe containers and for inspections. Documentation of each shipment arriving at the Station is checked and assistance given to UK Customs in checking CITES licences. All shipments are given individual attention: feeding, watering, cleaning and removal of dead or moribund and the sick and injured are given veterinary care. If there is a long delay between flights animals are released into appropriate pens when necessary. Inspectors prepare evidence for legal action in cases of maltreatment, substandard containers or poor loading.

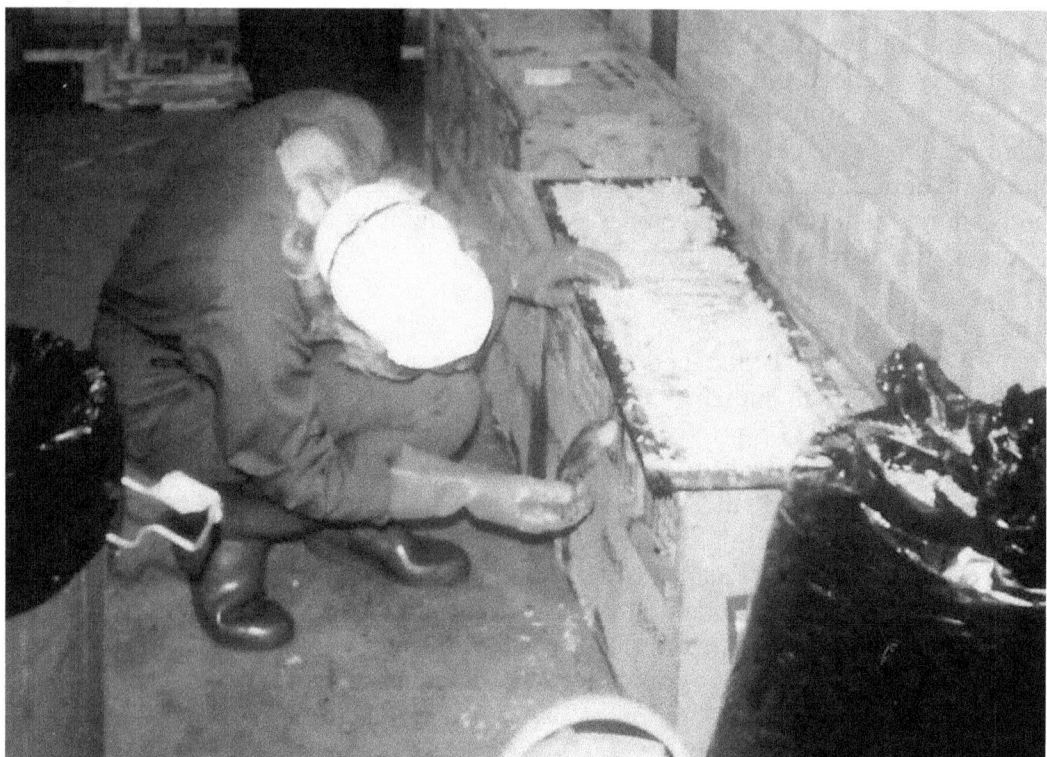

A monkey touchingly stretches out an arm for food and reassurance while being cared for on a short stopover at the AQS Heathrow Airport facility. (1982)

The staff have treated innumerable animals and birds suffering the effects of transport stress and shock, disease and injuries due to bad crating and poor shipment and saved many lives. Numerous animals have been re-crated at the airlines expense to conform with their own IATA Regulations and many legal prosecutions taken under the Transit of Animals (General) Order 1973, legislation that proved invaluable in enforcing better standards and made possible by having Inspectors permanently on call.

The UK Transit of Animals (General) Order, 1973

This legislation (now the Welfare of Animals (Transport) Order, 2006) has proved extremely successful in improving and maintaining adequate standards of shipment of live fauna by air at Heathrow Airport, London. The Order requires that crates are suitable for the species, soundly made, not overcrowded, and that 'Livestock' and 'Upright' labels are attached. It specifies protection of the animals from injury or suffering from any cause: that animals must receive adequate fresh air, and must be fed and watered at appropriate intervals including any waiting periods. The Order protects all species of fauna excluding man.

Under its terms 'the person(s) at the time' are liable for any offence and therefore airlines are responsible for compliance while shipments are within UK jurisdiction. At first there were a significant number of prosecutions with 51 successful prosecutions 1977-84 for flagrant cases of abuse with dozens of

Part of a consignment that included emus, grand electus parrots and various hornbills from Singapore to Brussels in a totally enclosed crate making inspection difficult (top and side removed in this picture). (1982)

written and verbal cautions and seizures of shipments pending re-crating or veterinary treatment.

Strict enforcement in conjunction with advice given to airlines on particular problems so as to secure a co-operative working relationship has resulted in some improvements in recent years and a reduction in poor shipping standards. Part of this is accounted for by a resultant avoidance of Heathrow Airport by some shippers and airlines.

Avoidance of Heathrow Airport

The cost of the AQS health and welfare services and the effectiveness of its inspectors in enforcing the law have resulted in the diversion of trade routes away from Heathrow. It appears that traders and perhaps some airlines take the view that rather than risk the extra expenses involved, or risk being compelled to conform to regulations and standards by prosecution, it is preferable to use trade routes that avoid Heathrow. Elsewhere, apparently, they experience no similar 'trouble'.

An Appendix I endangered young pygmy chimpanzee in transit from a Belgium animal dealer to the Medical academy in Warsaw for research purposes with misleading documentation could not unfortunately be seized.

A typical example of 'trouble', as defined by traders involved a consignment in transit from Singapore to Brussels which arrived at Heathrow by 'mistake' in September 1982. Three crates containing five emus, six grand Electus parrots, two Rhinoceros Hornbills, three Wrinkled Hornbills, four Rufous-necked Hornbills and one great Pied Hornbill were found in severely overcrowded and filthy conditions. All the birds were released from their containers and immediately proceeded to groom themselves. The four largest hornbills were contained in a totally enclosed crate with little ventilation, which was too small for them. They were cleaned, fed and watered and were detained pending arrival of regulation containers. The other birds were also attended to and redistributed in their original crates and continued on their journey. The other four birds were to follow on a later flight. On receiving them, the Belgian dealer telephoned the Station alleging that the four detained hornbills had been stolen and that he was contacting Interpol. He stated forcefully that his consignments were always routed to avoid Heathrow due to this sort of 'trouble'.

In 1983 a Malaysian based primate exporter stated that his UK partners had advised him to ship all USA destined consignments via Tokyo and San Francisco to New York to avoid Heathrow, even though this involved a longer journey via airports lacking facilities to care for them.

Another example involved shipments of cheetahs from Namibia routed via Heathrow to several destinations. Each shipment arrived in sub-standard crates with the cheetahs suffering from heat exhaustion due to inadequate ventilation. The crates were also dangerously unsafe and airline personnel on one occasion refused to unload them from the aircraft. South African Airways was constantly asked to supply new crates involving great expense. After four such shipments no more arrived, but a month later there was a report that two cheetahs arrived dead in Brussels in transit from Namibia in similar crates.

If standards of crating and welfare are to be improved and maintained worldwide it is important that all major airports should have facilities to care for live fauna otherwise such shipments should be banned. States should also introduce welfare legislation similar to the UK which should be adequately enforced so that traders and airlines cannot view any airport as "lenient". It is evident at the moment that live animal shipments are treated the same as inanimate freight.

Standards of Inspection at Points of Export and Import

In 1983, the authors visited Senegal, Kenya, India, Thailand, Singapore, Indonesia and the USA where the standard of inspection at points of export and import was investigated. This showed that none visited (including the UK) had an adequate procedure for inspection of CITES and IATA requirements. It was found that:

i. in most cases there were no enforcement or veterinary officers based permanently at airports. Many officers had to travel large distances to airports, often resulting in shipments being held for long periods;

ii. at airports where officers were based, they lacked facilities to examine the shipments adequately and because of the practical difficulties only cursory examinations were made;

iii. officers often worked office hours only and shipments could be exported or imported at night or weekends without examination;

iv. at most airports only a percentage exported were examined;

v. of the airports visited only Changi airport, Singapore and Heathrow had animal facilities operational and in both cases there is no requirement for all shipments to be examined;

vi. enforcement officers were not well versed in crating and welfare standards and problems existed in this respect;

vii. few countries had endangered species legislation and were forced to rely on Custom legislation, often resulting in wildlife officers having no adequate enforcement powers.

The practical and legislative difficulties experienced by enforcement officers at airports in attempting to enforce CITES requirements is resulting in loopholes. Substitution and smuggling of endangered species and species protected by national laws and the continual acceptance of sub-standard crating is common. It is essential that all CITES Party States give priority to the establishment of adequate and efficient inspection services if enforcement of CITES requirements are to be improved and effective.

There were many instances of animal smuggling attempts in the cabin of aircraft often with the cabin crew's knowledge and even aid such as a protected baby gibbon which the crew helped feed, a baby crocodile put in the overhead locker, baby parrots and in this example a rucksack full of snakes, tortoises and turtles.

Smuggling of Specimens

Even at major airports with strict border controls, animal smuggling attempts of endangered and non-controlled fauna appear to be commonplace. Experience at Heathrow Airport has shown that many individuals attempt to hide fauna on their person in the cabin of the aircraft. Such attempts are often thwarted by cabin crew or fellow passengers who spot something unusual, hear strange noises or actually notice the animal and report it. There have also been cases where animals carried in the cabin have been blatantly on show and cabin crew have assisted with feeding them without raising any alarm. Education of both passengers and air crew is vital.

There have also been many incidents where false compartments have been constructed into crates to secrete animals not mentioned on the manifest. These secret compartments often confine animals in spaces without sufficient ventilation of space.

The Wildlife Traders

The evidence of the present study on preparation and shipment practices needs consideration in the context of the nature and character of the trade.

In the absence of an international data system on traders that might prevent their indiscriminate dismissal as an undesirable group, impartial judgement is difficult. The general reputation of traders in live animals is poor; close familiarity with trade practices does little to improve it. The UK Pet Trade Association (PTA) with a minority trader membership, has stated that many traders would not be acceptable as members; and a representative of the US Pet Industry Joint Advisory Council (PIJAC) stated that he recognized the need of the industry to 'improve its image'.

The present numbers of wildlife importers and exporters is uncertain. The guesstimate of Domalain, a former trader (1977) was that the numbers of exporters supplying the world market was probably somewhat over 500. A number of traders have attempted to improve their 'image' by operating as pseudo zoological institutions or parks, purportedly concerned with 'saving' endangered species. As noted by Uruguay at the fourth meeting of CITES Parties (1983) it is difficult for exporting states to discriminate between bona fida and pseudo institutions when deciding to issue licensees.

The primary concerns of trader associations are with the protection and development of their commercial interests. This is legitimate provided that there is, with the protection of such rights, a sense of obligation to the environment and of duty to the rest of Society. However to trade in wildlife it appears necessary to have more business talent than professional competence.

Unlike official and non-governmental conservation and welfare organisations, traders have taken no active measures to initiate or promote conservation and health and welfare objectives. The function of traders is, simply to trade. At the fourth meeting of CITES (1983), Interpol stated that sixteen countries reported a large number of cases of illegal trade during the period 1979-81. In 1971, massive lucrative illegal trading in reptiles was uncovered in the USA, in which 27 persons were arrested and at least 160 others, including zoo employees and wildlife traders were involved. The case revealed smuggling from Australia, Central and South America into the US, with re-exports being sold to Japan, Denmark, West Germany, Netherlands and the UK; all parties to CITES. In 1984, following 3 years' investigations in the US, a worldwide multi-million dollar illegal market in birds of prey was uncovered. Many of those arrested were prominent leaders of national and state falconry associations. Half of the birds captured died during handling and trade.

In recognizing the successes of US enforcement agents it would be naive to suppose dealers and traders in Europe and Japan are any more reputable than those in the US. Indeed, in the above cited cases European and Japanese traders were involved in illicit trade with their US counterparts. The revulsion at the unethical conduct of many traders has inspired suggestions that the trade in wild animals should be banned. Although the prospects for this are not encouraging. New York State has set a notable precedent by instituting a ban on the importation of wild birds from September 1985. Recognizing the difficulties of banning the trade on an international basis, the authors have considered regulation rather than prohibition; but regulation carefully designed to further the essential needs of law enforcement officials working in the field.

Disease and Health Risks.

Consignments of imported birds and animals, in particular wildlife recently caught, pose risks to humans and other animals in contact with them during transport. They are potentially serious sources of disease to the livestock of the importing countries; the value of commercial trade in wildlife and the costs of controlling it need evaluation from this perspective.

Great caution is necessary in examining imported live specimens since the validity of health certificates is often suspect. Allegedly, some health certificates are forged; and cursory examination in some countries of export often makes them worthless. The major stresses inevitable with transport are a factor in rendering specimens more susceptible to disease.

Some diseased birds may be re-exported: both the UK and USA allow traders to do this when shipments are refused entry due to being carriers of infectious disease. In light of animal and human interests and CITES requirements which specify animals shall be transported in a humane manner, this option to re-export should be reviewed by health and conservation authorities. It is not responsible or humane for any State to permit diseased specimens refused entry to their own country to be re-exported and remain in trade.

Of 3,199,094 US bird imports during 1976-81, 176,519 (5.5%) were denied entry due to disease and were re-exported elsewhere or back to the country of origin (US Dept. of Agriculture figures). Since stress compounds the effects of disease, it is likely a large proportion of these birds failed to survive the return journey, during which they may have infected other shipments if mixed with them in airline cargo sheds. While traders' option in the US is allowed in the UK, diseased birds found in the UK have been destroyed in quarantine.

Some of 335 Amazon parrots refused entry to the US while suffering from Newcastle's Disease and re-exported to West Germany via Heathrow being a health risk to all those coming into contact with them. The parrots were shipped in extremely overcrowded, two-tiered crates without water or adequate food adding to the suffering of prolonged travel.

A recent, November 1982, incident illustrates the unwise use of the re-export option, as well as the time and expense incurred by authorities through traders being allowed to exercise it for commercial reasons. A shipment of 335 yellow-naped Amazon parrots and 12 Scarlet macaws were shipped, apparently by sea, from El Salvador to Mexico, and thereafter to Seattle, USA. The certificate with the birds stated they were transported in a humane way, and were disease free. In US quarantine the birds were found to be infected with Newcastle's disease. The importer exercised his right to re-export to a buyer in West Germany, to where they were sent via Heathrow London. There, airline handlers noted the appallingly bad crates, and saw that many birds looked sick. They reported this to the AQS, whose Inspectors examined the birds finding them grossly overcrowded in two tier crates, and that two immature macaws had badly deformed beaks preventing them from eating. There were no accompanying documents revealing their diseased status and re-export, but this was subsequently confirmed, although it was plain to see they were diseased. Government veterinary officials were called in and the birds released, fed and attended to under strict quarantine conditions. After inter-Governmental discussions, the West German authorities agreed to permit entry. In allowing such procedures both the UK and USA are placing IATA member airlines in the position of either refusing to carry them or violating IATA-LAR. In such

Two shipments consisting of 4,500 birds from Tanzania to Chicago diverted to Heathrow suffered 721 deaths by the time they reached London. The airline cargo driver refused an order to move them to their onward flight due to their terrible condition. A further 227 died at the Heathrow animal facility within two hours of arrival.

cases officials are constrained to act within the terms of the law and regulations that render them unable to act in terms of CITES.

Some diseases can be transmitted from animals and birds to humans (zoonosis); therefore, persons in close contact with specimens during transit, quarantine, or even after sale, can be at risk. One such zoonotic disease carried by birds is Psittacosis (Ornithosis), mainly found in parrot species; some less infectious strains are also found in pigeons and passerines. This is caused by *Chlamydia Psittaci,* an intracellular parasite. Humans become infected by inhaling contaminated airborne material through handling dead birds, or by being in close contact with infected birds or cages or material contaminated with excreta or nasal discharges. Clearly, airline personnel and transport workers may be subject to high risk in aircraft holds, cargo sheds or vehicles, where the caged birds flutter and panic spreading dust. Such workers at Heathrow were blissfully unaware of such hazards and were put at risk through lack of education or protection. In 1980 a shipment of Amazon parrots from South America infected with the disease, resulted in several airline personnel and animal attendants at the AQS being hospitalised in isolation for several weeks, two of them being critically ill at one point. There are many instances of deaths in the UK and US from psittacosis related infection from imported birds.

The following is a list of some of the disease and infection risks from contact with imported animals:

Rabies: Fatal, infectious viral diseases against which UK (and other countries) quarantine laws are designed to protect. Occurs in animals such as bats, dogs, cats and monkeys and man.

Leptospirosis (Weil's disease): spirochete (coiled rod-shaped bacterium) infection from contact with infected urine, excreta, soil or water of rodents, dogs and other mammals. Four animal attendants at Heathrow were seriously ill following such contact with a shipment of Cheetahs.

Tuberculosis: from the micro bacterium tuberculosis through inhalation in aerosol form when handling infected animals particularly primates.

Salmonellosis: occurs as the result of infection from a range of organisms of the Salmonella group affecting humans, mammals, birds and particularly reptiles.

Fungal infections: among the most common is Aspergillosis, a disease affecting animals.

Coliform infections: to varying degrees, most birds suffer from Escherichia coli, a bacterium affecting the gastro-intestinal tract and the respiratory system.

Newcastle's (Fowl Pest): an acute feverish and infectious viral disease from which import restrictions are designed to protect the UK, USA and other countries.

Hepatitis: occurs in animals and man. Caused by two or more viruses; transmissible by contact with infected excreta.

Tetanus: Occurs in animal and man from infection through a skin wound.

The IATA Live Animals Regulations Manual (IATA-LAR)

The IATA-LAR Manual is a valuable source of reference for whose development the Live Animals Board merits commendation. The present authors emphasise that, notwithstanding their criticisms, they consider it a valuable work.

Published for thirteen years it is now (1984) in its 11th. Edition. The number of IATA member airlines who should be adhering to the Regulations is 123. Another 90 participating airlines have agreed "to accept animals in accordance with the terms of these Regulations". The importance of the manual lies in its practical use, and the degree to which its terms and conditions are applied in practice. Equally, this applies also to the Articles of the CITES which specify: ' any living specimen will be so prepared and shipped as to minimise the risk to injury, damage to health and cruel treatment'. Years of experience suggest IATA-LAR 'minimum standards' are achieved more as an exception than the rule. Most live wild fauna shipments are carried in substandard conditions by CITES and IATA criteria.

The 11th. Edition of the guidelines is now a fairly substantial reference work of 250 pages, a notable increase on earlier editions. Constructively, it emphasizes attention to conservation and welfare requirements. In terms of daily practice however, it tends to remain on the shelves gathering dust. Valuable as a reference, then, the question arises whether in its present form it is achieving the practical purpose of ensuring the welfare of animals.

Java sparrows sit expectantly round water pots during a transit stop at AQS Heathrow. Overcrowding in confined spaces causes great heat build-up in the crates and dehydration in the birds and plentiful water is essential.

Particular points worth raising are:

- There is considerable repetition throughout which often has the effect of confusing rather than clarifying points;
- Specifications have always been open to varying interpretation which prevented standardisation;
- It appears questionable if the precise designs illustrated have been tested in ordinary working conditions and if the practicability for the trade to construct them has been tested.

The potentially valuable manual is too little used and it is necessary therefore to devise means of encouraging its use. This might be helped by making it:

i. More simple and explicit;
ii. More freely available to the actual exporters/traders, agents and others concerned with the trade;
iii. Crate designs, at least for specimens most frequently shipped, are available in cheaply produced leaflet form.

The main problem is that when airlines are confronted with a shipment of live fauna at the point of export, local conditions may make it impossible to refuse it should it be in substandard or non-regulation containers even if personnel had the confidence and knowledge to do so. Live animal shipments in general are viewed and treated just the same general inanimate freight and airlines do not like to turn away business or upset customers.

CITES Guidelines for the Transport of Live Wild Animals and Plants.

This booklet of 109 pages published in 1980, contains general information on the preparation and shipment of living specimens carried by all forms of transport. A commendable feature is that the Guidelines apply to all animals, not just those presently listed under the Convention. Broadly based on the IATA regulations the booklet offers 'guidelines only' in a form adaptable to local legislative requirements. The Guidelines are of little use in practical terms of the trade by air. IATA are more appropriate because they are more specific, despite this, even these are too little used. The care of animals in air transport is a rather specialist field, and with all due respect to the consultants involved, it appears few had first-hand daily experience with practical problems of animals by air. However the Guidelines may have served a useful purpose in directing attention of the Conference to the major problems encountered in the shipment of animals by air. The Conference decision to give qualified endorsement to IATA-LAR was more practical, notwithstanding that airline priorities need reconciling with those of CITES. Instead of general guidelines, the need was, and is, for the provision of information in simple, specific form, with clearly explicit crate designs and directions, aimed at persons actually handling consignments, as well as for enforcement officers.

Some Problems Concerning Practical Application of CITES Requirements.

Disposal of Seized Animals.

A major difficulty in the UK, as elsewhere, is the disposal of detained or seized animals. Some seized shipments may involve substantial numbers, particularly birds and reptiles. To find suitable accommodation is not simple. In countries such as the UK and USA, quarantine regulations complicate the issue. Zoos are often asked to hold or quarantine seized shipments and this may lead to animals being, through necessity, held in less than suitable conditions resulting in higher mortality rates. Incidents have occurred that make seizure or 'saving' of such animals farcical for enforcement officers. There is also the matter of subsequent disposal and completion of quarantine and legal action. This has resulted in zoos and others having unwanted animals which sometimes return into the trade.

Repatriation of Specimens.

Experience at Heathrow Airport has shown there can be practical difficulties in repatriating animals to their country of origin. The main problems are:

a) so far, no international agreements have laid down practical procedures for repatriating specimens; arrangements need time during which the animals require accommodation and care;

b) the question as to who pays for this accommodation and care, the possible need for fresh crates and veterinary attention, as well as the return flight cost, is unresolved. The difficulties of establishing intention on the part of the importers when shipments are seized poses further difficulties on fixing legal liabilities for such costs;

c) to whom are specimens to be returned? Release back into the wild may not always be feasible or advisable;

d) many specimens are unfit after a single journey, let alone two. The stresses involved during transport appears insufficiently appreciated;

e) the health certification and other documentation procedures, as well as import controls, would require some countries of origin to review existing procedures and requirements now preventing repatriation.

Disposals should benefit enforcement and administration of the Convention ensuring no gain to the Trade in general or any trader in particular. It is of equal importance that guilty importers and/or carriers of live specimens should meet costs of confiscation, custody and return of specimens to countries of origin. The suggestion that charitable and conservation groups should bear financial burdens for inadequate governmental provisions and violations of law by animal traders is unacceptable. It is the responsibility of traders, as of governments, to know national laws and regulations applying to the terms of the Convention.

The poorly organised international trade in live fauna already has been subsidised by governments and non-governmental organisations who, for many years have paid for its deficiencies. If the trade is to continue, the need for international regularization, via CITES, and the development of means to require traders to bear the costs of their own malpractices is essential. Pending rationalisation of the Trade it is possible that Parties should withhold permits from certain exporters whom have a proven record of irregular or negligent practice.

Endangered Species in Transit

Problems have been experienced at Heathrow Airport with suspect shipments of CITES Appendix species. Detention or seizure of specimens in transit from one country to another has been difficult without firm evidence of intent to smuggle or otherwise evade national controls under CITES. Smuggling of specimens in false compartments or wrongly identified were rare, possibly due to the reputation of the airport for having strict controls.

Several incidents did occur at the airport involving Appendix I species in transit from one non-CITES country to another. One widely publicised incident in 1979 involved an unweaned female lowland gorilla which originated in Cameroun and was shipped to an Austrian dealer who held it briefly before attempting to export it to Japan via Heathrow Airport. The gorilla was detained at the AQS on welfare grounds when it was discovered that it was travelling unaccompanied, requiring bottle feeding every four hours and was contained in a sub-standard crate. It was considered that the gorilla was too young to survive the long journey to

Japan. UK Customs were informed and it was detained for a week while the background to the transaction was investigated. Seizure of the Appendix I gorilla was found to be legally impossible and the gorilla was released from Custom detention, but I was not happy to allow its further unaccompanied shipment to Japan on welfare grounds. Eventually the poor creature was shipped back to Austria under special arrangements with a new comfortable crate provided. Unfortunately a few days later the gorilla was shipped to Japan via a route avoiding Heathrow. The documentation in this case did identify the animal correctly, although the dealer had signed an airline shipper's certificate stating that it was not an endangered species.

In another incident in 1982, an Appendix I young pigmy chimpanzee was seen in transit from a Belgium dealer to the Medical Academy in Warsaw. Believed to be destined for research, it was well crated and in sound condition, but circumstances again, did not allow for detention. The airline documents contained only the name of the shipper's agent and misleadingly referred to the animal as a 'monkey'. Airlines commonly fail to fully record the shipper's identity and whereabouts, and shippers often give brief, misleading descriptions. These matters are important in the event of legal and other difficulties during transit.

One successful case involved a young siamang gibbon, found in the hand baggage of a passenger in transit from Thailand to Spain. Intention to smuggle was accepted by UK Customs and the gibbon was seized and eventually transferred to an establishment specialising in the captive breeding and study of this species.
This type of incident shows the importance of:
➢ Airlines liaising fully with CITES and not accepting endangered species wrongly identified in documentation;
➢ Animal holding facilities in caring for detained animals which might not otherwise survive such holding periods or be sized in the first place;
➢ Welfare legislation in aiding enforcement of CITES.

Conclusions and Recommendations

Whatever the system devised it is clear there will always be a few traders engaged in illegal activity. A systematic revision of the Trade must start inevitably with the traders. For practical reasons it needs to begin in consumer countries: it is they who are the major cause of the problems; their politico-economic power and resources are overwhelming in relation to those of the main wildlife producer countries. Since the one who pays the piper calls the tune, it is the consumer countries who are calling the tune for the live wildlife trade, despite bans by some wildlife producers.

Liaison between Interested Groups

If the suffering and loss of life caused by the international trade in live wild specimens due to injury, damage to health and cruel treatment is to be prevented it is essential to achieve reciprocal co-operation and liaison between management authorities of the Parties, IATA, CITES Secretariat and Technical Committee and Non-Governmental Organisations (NGO's). The emphasis of such a group must be with standards of practice.

It is recommended that such liaison must include Government and Airline officials directly concerned with daily practical inspection and handling problems of the Trade. It should also include NGO's with direct, consistent, practical experience of the Trade.

With respect to the involvement of representatives of the trade, it is just to invite comments, evidence and objections from them on decisions and recommendations, but it is inappropriate for their representatives to take part in better policing.

Moratorium on the International Commercial Trade

Given reciprocal understanding and co-operation the appended recommendations and amendments to IATA Live Animal Regulations will present no major difficulties. Improved implementation however, will be far less simple and will require time to be developed.

Pending establishment of such procedures and with certain exceptions for non-commercial transactions, a partial moratorium on the international commercial trade in live specimens of fauna is justified.

Recommendations on the Revision and Amendment of the IATA Live Animals Regulations.

Some 245 recommendations on the amendment of Container notes and 60 specific amendments can be found in The Preparation and Shipment of Living Specimens of Wild Fauna Carried by Air. Being too numerous to mention in this excerpted report, the following general recommendations are covered here:

1. **Shipment of Pregnant Animals and Immature Specimens**: *No IATA member airline or participating carrier should accept pregnant females or females with un-weaned young or un-weaned young alone.*

2. **Food and Water Requirements**: Notes now stating *'may be provided'* must be replaced with *'must be provided'* and the statement that birds *'do not require feeding during the first 24 hours' must be deleted. No airline should accept live animal shipments without access to water and food and lacking the means or access to replenish them as necessary during transit.*

3. **Crate Design**: *Specific measurements for crates and the number of specimens they should contain need to be stated and researched.*

4. *A main aim of IATA/CITES should be, so far as possible, the standardisation of containers when-ever possible and based on amended designs.* Bearing in mind that certain live wild species are regularly shipped over established routes, IATA/CITES approved re-usable crates should be introduced.

5. *No airline should accept living specimens so crated that inspection by wildlife, customs and health and welfare officials is obstructed*. IATA/CITES should emphasise all crates are subject to inspection.

6. **Acclimatisation**: *IATA/CITES should advise airline carriers to require official certification that wild live specimens have been acclimatised to captivity for a period of not less than 28 days.*

7. **Airline Carrier Liabilities**: If IATA Regulations are to be enforceable insofar as airlines are concerned the presumption must be that, on acceptance, packing is not defective. *Liability by airlines must be accepted and disclaimers for liability for losses due to 'natural' causes should be reviewed.* Through IATA-LAR, airline carriers at present disclaim liability for defective packing and for mortality and injury.

8. **Routings**: *IATA should instruct carriers to route animal shipments, wherever possible, via airports with animal facilities or shortest routes in regard to flight time.* Such routings are of value to the monitoring and enforcement of CITES regulated species and health and welfare considerations, and would counter the deliberate avoidance of such facilities by traders.

9. **Airline Personnel Information and Education**: Awareness/informal material must be produced and distributed by IATA/CITES in conjunction with Unions and NGO's. Posters in the manner of work/safety warning notices must be designed and displayed in cargo facilities showing basic handling procedures. Container labels should be produced duplicating points emphasised on the posters. Cartoon/pictorial methods would eliminate the need for text in different languages.

10. **Species Not Suitable for Carriage**: *In conjunction with CITES,WTMU and the present authors, a list of species unsuitable for carriage should be compiled and include in IATA with the instruction that no carrier should accept such species except in non-commercial cases where Scientific Authorities are satisfied that special and adequate arrangements have been put in place.*

11. **Species Most Commonly Shipped**: *IATA container notes (with amendments recommended in this study), for species most commonly shipped, should be produced in leaflet form and made available to licensing, enforcement officers and exporters/importers.*

12. **The CITES Guidelines for Transport:** The guidelines state that '...these packers' guidelines have been designed to **obviate the inclusion** of any dimensions or specifications as to the precise materials that should be used

in the construction of containers'. And '**scope is given**..... to use suitable crates in such a manner that they are suitable for the size and number... [of specimens]'. (Authors' emphasis). Such phrases encourage the causes of most of the problems as everything becomes ambiguous and open to personal interpretation. ***The Guidelines should be reviewed in this context.***

13. **Preparation and Shipment Requirement Sheets:** ***There should be liaison on preparation and shipment affairs between CITES, IATA and the Parties to produce sheets that inform applicants it is their prior duty to conform with specific Container Note requirements, that specimens had been acclimatised to captivity and in signing these sheets, exporters would undertake to conform with these requirements.*** The sheets would accompany other shipping documents. CITES export certificates should also include a crating, health and welfare checklist to be completed and signed by official inspectors prior to shipment stating that crates are suitable, that food and water is available and that all specimens are visible and not overcrowded.

14. **Education of Enforcement Officers:** ***Video and slide presentations should be available covering crating and welfare standards and other topics mentioned in this Report which can be used to instruct airline and official enforcement officers.***

15. **Convention Article III para 3(b):** This Article specifies that for Appendix I listed specimens the 'Scientific Authority of the State of import' (should be) 'satisfied the recipient of a living specimen is suitably equipped to house and care for it'. ***Species listed on Appendices II and III as well as species not listed by CITES appendices should also be included in this paragraph.*** This is consistent with the ruling of the Parties on the Care and Shipment of Living Specimens and should apply to **all** species.

16. **Convention Clauses to cover specimens in Quarantine:** The same Convention clauses referring to protecting living specimens from harm should also be relevant for specimens undergoing quarantine. As far as the UK and USA are concerned, living specimens are not permitted to enter the domestic trade until the quarantine period is completed. This implies that during this period they may be regarded as still in international trade. ***The Convention clauses should cover the quarantine or holding period.***

17. **Re-export of diseased specimens:** In light of human and animal health interests, re-export of diseased specimens should be reviewed by health and conservation bodies.

18. **Responsibility for costs of re-exported or confiscated specimens:** Disposals should only benefit the enforcement and administration of the CITES Convention and not the trade in general or any trader in particular.

To this end guilty importers/exporters should meet the costs of confiscation, custody and return of specimens.

19. **Repatriation and Holding of Confiscated Specimens:** Considerable problems have been experienced worldwide in the holding and repatriation of confiscated animals back to the country of origin. Often, enforced use of sub-standard holding premises have resulted in the death or suffering of many animals. *It is recommended that urgent action is taken to alleviate this situation.*

20. **The Need for Airport Animal Holding Facilities:** There is a proven indispensable need for adequate and specialised facilities for holding and caring for animal's at all major air and sea ports where large numbers of live fauna are transhipped or imported/exported. *CITES/IATA should urge the establishment of such centres and the international trade should be restricted to such ports.*

21. **Restricted Ports of Entry**: *All countries should restrict the designated ports of entry to the minimum and preferably to those ports with the facilities to handle and care for them.*

22. **Standards of Enforcement of Welfare Legislation**: *All Party States should adopt welfare legislation similar to that of the UK Transit of Animals (General) Order 1973*, (now the Welfare of Animals (Transport) Order 2006). *Such legislation should be strictly enforced to counter the use of more 'lenient' airports by the trade.*

23. **Welfare Conditions at Traders Holding and Quarantine Premises**: If Parties to CITES are genuine in wishing to seriously treat the Conventions requirements on preparation and shipment standards, the following is recommended:

   a) *that Authorities responsible for veterinary health and welfare need to exercise more stringent supervision over welfare standards at traders' premises;*
   b) *that national enforcement systems need specialised inspectors with no reliance on importers/exporters whatsoever and with aviculturist and zoological competence in assessing standards of welfare;*
   c) *that prospective importer/exporters of live fauna need to provide evidence of such knowledge, experience and competence in caring properly for captive wild fauna;*
   d) *that traders who continually receive consignments sustaining high mortalities either in transit or within the period of holding/quarantine should have their licences suspended following investigation.*

The present study has shown that with respect to the trade in live specimens by air:
  a) IATA Live Animal Regulations are in need of review and amendment to be consistent with the terms of CITES;
  b) that airlines generally do not enforce IATA-LAR in practice, that IATA and airlines are able to co-operate with enforcement agencies, but cannot be expected to perform an enforcement role other than is consistent with their business interests;
  c) that while IATA-LAR, suitably amended, may establish satisfactory standards, these are meaningless without action by Parties to enable the Regulations to be applied in practice;
  d) that the responsibility for preparation and shipment is with the traders;
  e) that, generally, the traders cannot be deemed to meet the requirements of CITES or IATA in this regard;
  f) that unacceptable high mortalities occur as the result of practices by traders and airlines causing injury, damage to health and cruel treatment harmful to the conservation purposes of the Convention;
  g) that more effective action is needed, and is possible, to repair existing deficiencies;
  h) that wildlife importer/consumer countries should initiate remedial action since their demand is the major cause of the trade and have the resources necessary for such action.

Addendum

Release of the report resulted in widespread coverage in the UK national newspapers, radio and TV and coverage in animal welfare orientated publications and airline trade magazines. It caused a hornet's nest of acrimony amongst everyone connected with the trade and most closed ranks to denounce and dismiss it, as if embarrassed by its findings and their lack of action in doing something about the situation. Everyone was quick to discount the report as "out of date" when in fact the suffering and mortalities continued for another two decades despite increasing evidence and research. A similar report in 1991 was still cataloguing cases of shipments with high mortality and suffering from all parts of the world to Europe (*RSPCA 1991*).

Air Cargo News International, gave massive coverage of the report in their May 15 and June 12 1985 issues which was very helpful in educating and bringing the issue to the attention of airline staff. UK national newspapers such as the Daily Express, Daily Mirror and The Times among others covered the report extensively.

Graham Joss, MRCVS the veterinary advisor and a spokesman for the IATA Live Animals Board when interviewed on BBC Radio 4 'World at One' programme about the report appeared to blame everyone except the airlines. He stated that "*unfortunately, very often when you go back right down the line, you find that somebody may have even been bribed to accept these* [bad shipments]" and that the airlines "*do not have the power to refuse or make certain these* [IATA] *regulations are carried out."* Incidentally airlines of course have the power to refuse shipments. Discussing why shipments are accepted in poor crating he stated *"it's not in their* [airlines] *interest to refuse them"*. He commented that veterinary surgeons in the exporting countries signed export certificates without examining the shipments and that the report authors should go over to the exporting countries and resolve it. At no time did he suggest that in the interests of animal welfare, which as a vet should have been his main concern, live animal shipments should be banned particularly from countries with a poor record. He attacked the report in another press statement commenting he *"had never heard of the group"*. Vic Attwood, Chairman of IATA Live Animals Board commented that *"many of the cases mentioned in the report are now historic and have been previously well documented,"* even though all of the incidents mentioned had never been publicised before.

The City of London Animal Quarantine Station (AQS) also hit out stating *"We would not deny that these horrific events did happen, but the report is based on happenings during 1979-83 and it is out of date"* and *"airlines have instigated immense improvements in the last two years"* (*Skyport 1985*). It was rather curious that suddenly after decades and without any reason, such great improvements had been made which was obviously not the case, but they wanted to distance themselves from any criticism. Although complimentary about their brilliant work, of which the authors were part, we were not welcomed at the facility following the report.

Incidents and prosecutions still continued belying these statements including a £20,000 fine and £5,000 costs against KLM in 1990 regarding a consignment of 8,000 birds from Tanzania which suffered 1,200 deaths (*RSPCA 1991*).

Surprisingly many animal conservation and welfare groups also came out against the report appearing to be embarrassed by its findings. The RSPCA had long operated an animal facility at Heathrow which had been superseded by the AQS as it was not up to standard, stated at the time that conditions had improved and their services were no longer required. Although having performed wonderful work over several decades caring for and saving many animals they had done little to tackle the overriding problem. The RSPCA Chief Veterinary Officer at the time in a conversation with the author also dismissed the report as out of date and troublemaking. In 1991 though, the RSPCA belatedly decided to take more interest in the issue, publishing a report written by EIA. The RSPB following their reports in 1975/6 remained relatively quiet on the issue.

The august Fauna and Flora Preservation Society (FFPS) with a plethora of scientific Vice-Presidents and experts seemed upset that they were not consulted before publication and thought the report *"full of errors of interpretation and woolly definitions, containing no references or sources"* and pompously *"that the authors were 'naive' and did not have "enough experience"* (*Burton 1985*). They also stated naively that *"it is mainly concerned with animal welfare, not relevant to CITES"*, even though the title of the report was based on the CITES principle that all animals should be transported in conditions preventing cruelty and suffering. They even attacked Sir Peter Scott (who was FFPS President at the time) for his Foreword to the report. All failed to realise that the report contained all new research and photographs never seen before based on years of actual frontline experience.

Aviculturists, animal traders and their trade magazines such as Cage and Aviary Birds heavily and cynically criticised Sir Peter and the report by letter and articles, obviously in support of the trade and its continuance, dismissing most of the findings and doing whatever they could to delay bans or changes that would affect the perpetuation of the trade.

The UK Government, although a signatory to CITES showed no sign of taking any interest in the issue and was also dismissive and completely uncooperative, refusing to allow access or provide details of the mortality of birds and animals in quarantine to further our research for the benefit of the animals, although they did allow access to ten sample records of bird quarantine. The Swedish and Danish Governments by comparison did allow the author access to their quarantine records which together with the sample UK records and those from the USA proved that high mortality did occur in the first few weeks following importation.

What the Report Achieved

As a consequence of our report, a CITES Working Group was set up to study the transport conditions of live fauna. Although the authors and EIA's research and recommendations was a focal point of discussions by the Working Group and the Live Animals Board (LAB) of IATA and every effort was made to assist, we were ultimately excluded.

The report recommended 245 individual amendments to the IATA Live Animal Regulations specifying particular changes to crate designs, sizes, numbers per crate, food and water facilities, methods of carriage, handling and loading of which 102 were incorporated, although it was still insufficient to ensure the welfare of the animals.

At the 1987 (6th) and 1989 (7th) CITES conferences, a resolution was passed calling for the closer control of transport conditions for live animals covered by CITES including a checklist requiring minimum standards for containers, feeding, watering and documents to be completed prior to shipment.

In 1990, Lufthansa the world's leading wild bird carrier at the time banned the carriage of wild caught bird shipments stating *"We have a moral obligation to avoid this immense animal suffering caused by the transport of exotic birds"*.

In 1992 the USA banned the import of wild-caught exotic birds, but it wasn't until July 2007 that the European Union finally agreed to ban their import, not for welfare reasons, but fears of the spread of avian disease. By this time though, the trade had dropped from 7.5 million birds in 1975 to 1.5 million in 2006 and it was too late for all the countless millions of birds which had died during the decades of apparent indifference to the trade. Although welcomed by animal welfare groups it was incongruously criticised by CITES.

I believe our report helped kick start serious discussion and interest in the plight of wild animals during capture, transport and quarantine holding which culminated eventually in bans and better conditions. Unfortunately for many animals and birds it took far too long for all sides involved in the argument to do the right thing.

John Brookland (2016)

The authors would like to thank the following people for their valuable cooperation, insight and hospitality during our visits to their countries:

The Gambia
Mr E Brewer, Director, Wildlife Conservation Division

Senegal
Mr Sen, Director, Secretariat d'etat aux Eaux & Forets.
Mr Foul, Secretariat d'etat aux Eaux & Forets.
Mr Rahmane Gueye, Interpreter.
Mrs & Mrs L Diallo, Viv Anim (bird exporter).
Mr Boubou Wade, Oisellerie fauna Senegalaise (Bird exporter).
Mr A Diallo (bird exporter).

Kenya
Mr Oriero, Director, National Parks.
Mr Pertet, Asst. Director, Research & Management, National Parks
Mr & Mrs D Hunt, Mount Kenya Game Ranch
Mr K Hunt, Mount Kenya Game Ranch
Mr R Mann, (Primate exporter)
Mrs P Widdowson, Executive Officer, KSPCA
Mr J Richardson, MRCVS
Mr E Monks, Elsa Trust

India
Mr S K Mukherjee, Asst. Director, Dept of Wildlife, Delhi
Chief Enforcement Officer, Delhi
Mr P C Roychoodh, Asst. Director, Calcutta
Chief Enforcement Officer, Calcutta
Mrs Wright, WWF, Calcutta
Dr Tikader, Zoological Survey of India
Mr R Sarup, British airways, Delhi Airport
Pan Am Airlines, Delhi
Lufthansa Airlines, Delhi
Mr D Ram, (bird exporter)
Mr Mukherjee, Asian Birds and Animals, (exporter)

Thailand
Mr P Suvanakorn, Director, Wildlife Conservation Division, Bangkok
Mr B Ankhasirichinda, Chief of Protection Section, Wildlife C D
'Chiwan', Wildlife Enforcement Officer
'Jang', Wildlife Conservation Division
Mr A Tirawatana, Chief Wildlife Control centre, Don Muang Airport
Duty Veterinary Officer, Don Muang Airport
Mr P Round, Assoc. for Conservation of Wildlife (ACW)

Dr Boonsang (ACW)
Mr C Youngprapakorn, Samutprakan Crocodile Farm
Mr K Nukulphanichwipat, Siam Farm & Zoological Co Ltd
Mr Wirot Nutaphand, Siam Farm and Zoo.

Malaysia
Mr Mohammed Khan, Dir. General, Dept. of Wildlife
Mrs Ibrahim, Dept. of Wildlife, Kuala Lumpur
Mrs Halimah Muda, Dept. of Wildlife, Selangor
Mr E Laursen, Research Primates
Bird exporter (name not divulged)

Singapore
Dr Siew Teck Woh, Director, Primary Production Dept.
Dr J Koh, Veterinary Officer, Primary Production dept.
Dr N Nair, Veterinary officer, City Veterinary Centre
Mr Low Keng Hock, Animal Hostel, Changi Airport
Mrs Marjorie Doggett, IPPL/WSPA
Mr Liao Khoon Ngain, Singapore Airport Terminal Services
Mr Teo Ching Kang, Changi International Airport Services
Mr T Loh Peck Soon, Universal Tropical Enterprises, (exporter)

Indonesia
Mr H Rochim, Garuda Airlines, Jakarta Airport
Mr A Darmawan, CV Inquatex, exporter
Wildlife Officers, Halim International Airport

USA
Ms D Petrula, Mr B Schaff & Mr R Drifka, Wildlife Inspectors, Fish & Wildlife, Los Angeles Airport
Dr Shirley McGreal, International Primate Protection League

United Kingdom
Wildlife Trade Monitoring Unit, IUCN: Messrs J Barzdo, T Inskipp, C Huxley.
WSPA: Mr C Platt
IPPL: Mr C Rosen

Sources/Further Reading

Air Cargo News International (1985), *Scandal of the Airfreight Animal Killers*, 15th.May p1,8,9,10 & 11

Bates, J (1985) Row breaks out over live animal shipments, *Skyport,* 4th. April.

BBC Radio 4 (1985) Transcript of interview with Graham Joss, MRCVS, *World at One programme* 28th. March

Brookland, J, Hora, C. & Carter, N (1984): *The Preparation & Shipment of Living Specimens of Wild fauna in International Trade Carried by Air'* Authors & EIA

Brookland, J. & Carter, N (1986): *'Questions on the Handling of Live Wildlife Imports to the United Kingdom in Relation to Infectious Disease Hazards to Airline, Airport and HM Customs Personnel'* EIA

Brookland, J. & Carter, N. (1987): *Further Studies on the Preparation & Shipment of Wild Fauna – Imports to Denmark & Sweden in relation to CITES & IATA-LAR with Comparisons of mortality rates among wild bird shipments between Denmark, Sweden, UK and USA. EIA*

Brookland J: (1984 & 2016) *Airborne Animals-Cruelty in the Skies*

Burton, J. (1985) FFPS letter to EIA 11th. April & letter to Animal Welfare Institute 22nd. May

Byles, B (1985) On the Wing, *Cage & Aviary Birds,* 15th. June

Carter, N & Currey, Brookland, J. (1987): *The Trade in Live Wildlife, EIA*

Fitzgibbon, J. (1985) Reply to Sir Peter Scott's letter, *Cage & Aviary Birds,* 25th.

May & Letter to Editor, (1985) *Cage & Aviary Birds,* 10th. April.

Flight to Freedom – Wild Caught Birds, the Facts Behind the Trade, RSPCA Wildlife Department Report (May 1991)

Letters Page (1985) *Cage & Aviary Birds,* 25th.May, 8th. & 15th.June

Rees, A (1985) Scandal of the Flying Animals, *Daily Express,* 28th. March

Scott, Sir P. (1985) Letter to Editor, *Cage & Aviary Birds,* 3rd. May

 INTERNATIONAL UNION FOR CONSERVATION OF NATURE AND NATURAL RESOURCES

UNION INTERNATIONALE POUR LA CONSERVATION DE LA NATURE ET DE SES RESSOURCES

Conservation Monitoring Centre — Centre de surveillance continue de la conservation de la nature

Our ref: CRH/VII.1/vg

21 July 1982

<u>To whom it may concern</u>

This is to certify that Mr. John Brookland is, for the purposes of conducting a study of the capture, handling and international transportation of wildlife in relation to standards of CITES and IATA, an Honorary Consultant to the Wildlife Trade Monitoring Unit of the Conservation Monitoring Centre of the International Union for Conservation of Nature and Natural Resources.

I should be most grateful if you would assist and co-operate with Mr. Brookland as much as possible in the course of this study.

Wildlife Trade Monitoring Unit
219c Huntingdon Road, Cambridge CB3 0DL
Telephone: (0223) 277427

C.R. Huxley
Head, Wildlife Trade Monitoring Unit

219(c) Huntingdon Road, Cambridge CB3 ODL, United Kingdom Telex 817036 Cables: Redbook Cambridge UK
Tel: (0223) 277314 and 277420 (Species Conservation Monitoring Unit), 277427 (Wildlife Trade Monitoring Unit)

www.ingramcontent.com/pod-product-compliance
Lightning Source LLC
Chambersburg PA
CBHW081117280526
45787CB00007B/2865